A beginner's guide to sharemarket success

Shares
made simple

T0335160

Roger Kinsky

Wrightbooks

First published 2010 by Wrightbooks
an imprint of John Wiley & Sons Australia, Ltd
42 McDougall Street, Milton Qld 4064

Office also in Melbourne

Typeset in 11.5/13.4 pt Berkeley

National Library of Australia Cataloguing-in-Publication data:

Author:	Kinsky, Roger.
Title:	Shares made simple: a beginner's guide to sharemarket success / Roger Kinsky.
ISBN:	9781742469799 (pbk.)
Notes:	Includes index.
Subjects:	Stocks.
	Stock exchanges.
	Investment analysis.
Dewey Number:	332.642

Printed in Australia by McPherson's Printing Group

10 9 8 7 6 5 4 3 2 1

Disclaimer

The material in this publication is of the nature of general comment only, and does not represent professional advice. It is not intended to provide specific guidance for particular circumstances and it should not be relied on as the basis for any decision to take action or not take action on any matter which it covers. Readers should obtain professional advice where appropriate, before making any such decision. To the maximum extent permitted by law, the author and publisher and the owner of any material referred to or sourced in the material disclaim all responsibility and liability to any person, arising directly or indirectly from any person taking or not taking action based upon the information in this publication.

Contents

Preface

My first book about shares, *Online Investing on the Australian Sharemarket*, was well received by readers and is now in its third edition. After writing it, I felt there was a need for another book about shares that would allow readers to self-learn by including many worked examples and self-test exercises with solutions provided, so I wrote *Teach Yourself About Shares*. This book was also well received and has been reprinted a number of times. Encouraged by these successes, I decided to write another book that outlined the basic principles of share investing in a way that every reader would understand by making the explanations as simple as possible and by including only the amount of information needed for readers to be successful. In a nutshell, this book was written for readers who have the following preferences:

⇨ You'd like to invest successfully in shares for the long term and increase your wealth to the level you require for a comfortable life.

⇨ You want a low-stress approach to shares, where you avoid disasters and where you won't lose sleep worrying about your shares.

⇨ You don't want to pay a financial adviser or manager a fee for advice or to manage your share investments for you — you want to take control of your own financial destiny with confidence.

⇨ You don't want to spend a huge amount of time and effort learning all the ins and outs of the sharemarket in an attempt to become an expert.

⇨ You don't want to spend all day glued to a computer screen trading and following market trends.

In other words, if you want sole control of your financial destiny with shares and you want to use a simple, proven system based on sound investing principles that will maximise the probability of success, then this book is for you.

Every effort has been made to ensure the book is free of errors but in the real world perfection is difficult to achieve. I welcome feedback from readers who may have any constructive comments or suggestions for improvement. Please email me at <rkinsky@bigpond.com> or <rkinsky1@bigpond.com>, or contact John Wiley & Sons, who will forward any correspondence to me. I will promptly reply to any emails or letters I receive.

Finally, I'd like to wish you every success in your share investing, and I trust that this book will guide you in this direction.

Roger Kinsky
Woollamia, NSW
May 2010

Acknowledgements

I would like to thank CommSec for giving permission to reproduce charts and web pages included in this book.

Acknowledgement

chapter 1

Introduction to shares

In this chapter I'll outline the basic purpose of this book and also discuss some fundamental share investing principles and factors affecting the sharemarket, to lay the groundwork for the chapters that follow.

The scope of this book

If you'd like to invest successfully in shares without relying on the expertise of others and you don't want to spend lots of time on research or management of a share portfolio, then this book is for you. My aim is to show you how you can make a success of share investing in the simplest and least time-consuming way possible.

In this book I'll discuss investing in Australian shares only. I won't consider exchange-traded options, CFDs, forex, futures and suchlike, as they're strictly for high-risk investors who are prepared to spend a great deal of time and effort on trading and research. I won't discuss managed funds because they're controlled by others and there are management fees involved. Global shares require a high level of expertise and involve additional risk, so they're also excluded.

I'll make the explanations as simple as I possibly can with the least amount of jargon. But if jargon or special terminology can't be avoided, I'll explain all the terms I use. In other words, I'll start from square one and assume you know very little about shares.

Going your own way

Over the many years that I've written books about share investing and conducted share investing courses, I've received a great deal of feedback from readers and participants. These discussions have convinced me that there are many people who regard shares as a good investment but who lack the confidence and knowledge they think they'll need to become a successful investor. Consequently they use the services of a financial adviser or manager, who may be a person or investment organisation, that provides an investment service for clients. Some invest in a managed fund or allocated pension where the investment service is built into the investment product as a team of people with financial expertise manages the fund's capital. Others subscribe to a newsletter or tip sheet that contains research information and recommendations, or pay for a whiz-bang computer program or system that's been developed by some financial guru.

Naturally enough, whatever the choice there'll be a substantial fee for the service provided. When the advice or system produces good profits most investors accept that the fees and charges are necessary and they don't object to paying them. But when the profitability is low or negative, there's an investor backlash. The question they ask is: 'Why should I pay a substantial fee for a service that loses money?'

Part of the problem arises from the fact that financial advisers and fund managers cream off a management fee irrespective of the result of their efforts. Most often, fees are based on the amount of capital invested and bear no relation to the profitability of the investment. I think most investors would prefer incentive-based fees calculated as a percentage of the profits. After all, you're paying for advice to improve your profitability, and if the advice you receive doesn't do that, why should you pay? Financial advisers and fund managers will point out that frequently a drop in profitability is due to factors beyond their control (such as world events) but this problem can be easily overcome simply by linking the fee structure to a nominated market index.

A reader of my online investing book emailed me recently, and a comment he made expresses this sentiment very well: 'After a bitter and expensive experience with my high-profile financial adviser over the last ten years, I've decided to have a go myself'.

Investor backlash came to the fore during the financial crisis that hit the world in 2008–09, triggered by the sub-prime mortgage debacle in the US, when many investors were still paying substantial management fees even when their invested wealth eroded by 50% or even more.

Tip

You can become a successful share investor without rely-ing on the expertise of others.

My experience with options

Some time prior to the 2008–09 global financial crisis, I had a similar experience that convinced me self-management of my investments was the best way to go. Over some years, I had accumulated a substantial share investment portfolio that I successfully managed myself. To further boost my profits, I contemplated writing options over some of the shares I owned. I'd never done so before, so I decided to use the services of a respected investment organisation to gain experience in writing options before attempting to go it alone. The organisation assured me that writing covered options (as they're called) was the safest way of trading options, and they were confident that they could boost my share investing profits by writing options over shares they selected from my portfolio.

As it turned out, after the first year the options they wrote lost money and my share investing profitability was less than it would have been had I not been involved in options trading. Needless to say, as well as the loss on the options I still had to pay a substantial fee that increased the overall loss. When I queried the loss, I was told that a year was too short a period and that I had to persevere for a longer time. In the next year the result was the same, but the excuse this time was that the year had been an exceptional one and not good for options writing. To add to my annoyance, the market had risen during the year but the options they wrote lost money because of this! I was silly enough to persevere for another two years while they continued to lose money for me, until finally I'd had enough of the excuses and pulled the plug. As a final insult to injury I was then charged an additional substantial amount to close out the options they'd written that had not yet expired. This experience reinforced my belief that it's best to control one's own financial destiny and not rely on others.

Time and effort

As well as the investors who lack confidence based on the belief that they don't have the necessary knowledge to successfully manage their own investment in shares, there are many other investors who simply don't have the necessary time to do so. It's rather like mowing the lawn: many people are able to use a mower but would rather pay someone else to cut the grass for them. After all, it does take time to plan and manage an investment in shares and there are other things in life apart from financial gains.

Studies aimed at measuring personal happiness or satisfaction with life consistently show that of all the factors contributing to a person's psychological wellbeing, wealth is nowhere near the top of the list. Some of the more important factors are:

⇨ having a partner in a satisfying and loving relationship

⇨ being part of a family network, including children and grandchildren

⇨ being a member of a social network of friends and acquaintances

⇨ having a satisfying and meaningful occupation

⇨ participating in pleasurable hobbies and activities.

So let's face it, not everyone wants to spend all their free time glued to a computer screen trying to make share trading profits when there are so many other factors of importance in life. Everyone has a limited amount of time and it's necessary to prioritise the time that's available.

In my own case, my aim has always been to have enough wealth to be able to enjoy a comfortable lifestyle, but I see no point in accumulating wealth for wealth's sake. By comfortable lifestyle I mean being able to provide for the necessities of life for myself and my loved ones, with enough left over to buy the material possessions I'd like in order to support my lifestyle.

Can you beat the market?

At this point you might think, 'if I don't have a high degree of financial expertise and I'm not prepared to invest a great deal of time and effort into my share investing, surely I won't get superior returns'. So let's look at the question of how easy it is to beat the market and obtain superior returns.

There's a well-researched theory (that's not often discussed by those making a profit from providing share trading expertise) known as the efficient market theory (or hypothesis). This theory states that there's no possibility (other than by pure luck) of any person or system consistently being able to obtain share investing returns superior to those of the general market.

You can obtain insight into this theory by looking at what might happen if you play a poker machine. You could put several dollars into the machine and hit the jackpot, then stop playing and walk away with a big profit. However, if you continue playing, eventually you'll put all your winnings back into the machine and you'll walk away a loser because the machine is programmed in such a way that in the long run it pays out only a percentage of what's put in. The same type of scenario could occur when you first start share trading—your first few trades could be lucky ones and you might make a good profit. But if you keep trading long enough, the luck factor will go out of the equation and long-term probabilities will set in. If the efficient market theory is right, then it's unlikely that you'll be able to beat the market consistently.

When you really think about it, it's improbable (or even impossible) that the shares in a company will outperform the market over the long term. Consider the hypothetical situation I've illustrated in figure 1.1, where the share price of a listed company is outperforming the market.

Figure 1.1: share price outperformance

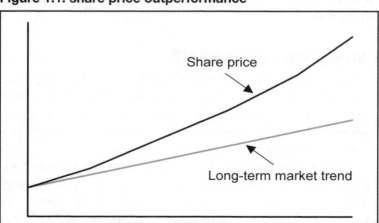

Can this scenario continue indefinitely? Experience indicates that this won't be so, and at some time in the future there's going to be a correction and the price will fall back, as illustrated in figure 1.2.

Figure 1.2: share price correction—typical scenario

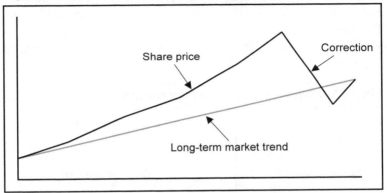

The price mightn't fall below the market trend before moving up again as I've illustrated, but there will inevitably be some correction. Of course, investors holding the shares long term won't be unduly concerned when there's a price fall as their shares are still doing as well as the general market, but those who bought in around the price peak might need to wait a long time before their shares show a capital gain again.

Tip

Beware of buying shares whose price has dramatically outperformed the overall market. There's bound to be a correction.

Average market performance

Another point to consider is that the market as a whole reflects the performance of all listed companies. However, in any time period some shares will perform better than others.

For example, if the average market return in one year is 10% (capital gains and dividends), that doesn't mean that all shares returned 10%. Far from it; some shares will be stellar performers and may return 100% or more, whereas others may be 'dogs' (apologies to all canines but that's the common sharemarket terminology) and investors could lose 50% or even 100% (you lose all your invested capital in these shares). I've illustrated this as a hypothetical performance curve for a year when the average market return was 10%, as shown in figure 1.3.

Figure 1.3: hypothetical market performance

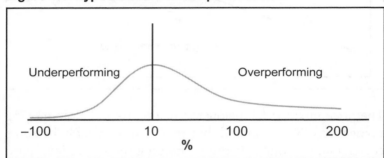

The average performance of 10% is shown by the vertical line; shares underperforming the market are to the left of this line and the overperformers are to the right. So it would seem that you can beat the market by getting onboard the ones that are outperforming the market and avoiding the underperformers. While that is unquestionably true, the problem with this philosophy is as I've already outlined. Outperformers seldom stay so consistently over a long period, and indeed this year's winners are often next year's losers and this year's losers are often next year's winners. And you can't tell that shares in a particular company are outperforming the market until some time after their outperformance becomes clear. By the time you jump onboard, the shares may have already reached their zenith and could soon start to track down.

Tip

There's no way of knowing that a share is outperforming the market until some time after the outperformance has begun. By then, it may be too late.

The market is always right

Suppose you entered a quiz show and you were pitted against an opponent who was never wrong. What would be your chances of winning? You might keep pace for a while but in the long run you'd eventually give a wrong answer and lose. Essentially this is the scenario when you try to consistently beat the market. To see why, consider the following two rules:

Rule 1: The market is always right.
Rule 2: If the market appears wrong, refer to rule 1.

How can this be so? The reason is the value of any commodity depends upon what a willing buyer will pay for it. This is known as the market value, and it's the true value of all commodities or assets, whether they be antiques, bottled water, bananas, property or shares. And since the market determines the price of shares, the market must always be right! Let's now consider an example.

An example

A well-respected broker sends you a report about XYZ company that examines its assets and liabilities, product sales and profitability, management, strengths and weaknesses, opportunities and threats, and concludes that based on all this research the shares in the company have a 'true' or 'intrinsic' worth of $1. However, when you check share prices you see that the shares in XYZ company are trading for $1.50. You'll most likely consider that the shares are overpriced and that the market has got it wrong.

A friend tells you that he's just bought shares in XYZ company. You tell him that he's made a mistake, the company is overpriced and you wouldn't pay more than $1 for the shares because that's their true value. However, the market's in a bull phase and several months later the shares are trading at $2. Your friend sells his shares and tells you gleefully that he's made a 33% return on his trading capital in a few months.

Later the bears take over and the price falls. Eventually the shares trade for $1, and now you decide to buy the shares—and guess what? The price continues to fall. When it reaches 80¢ you sell to minimise your losses.

In this scenario, your friend made a good profit by following the market trend and you made a loss because you felt the market was wrong and you refused to follow the trend the market indicated.

Contrarian investing

Now don't get me wrong, I'm not advocating that you blindly follow the market even when you feel shares are overpriced or underpriced but the market is doing the opposite. Trading against market trends is known as contrarian investing and in some cases can work very well. For example, Warren Buffett (who's widely regarded as the most successful investor in the world) refused to follow the market during the technology boom because he didn't understand what these companies were doing and he never invests in a business he doesn't understand. He missed a lot of profits that some investors made in the short term, but he was vindicated in the long term when the tech boom turned into a tech wreck and many investors lost huge amounts.

In the long run, the market will usually come to its senses and share prices will reflect some sort of 'true value'; that is, a price that's in some way related to the real value of the shares based upon profitability and assets. But it might take a long time to do so, and in the meantime profits are made or lost according to the dictates of the market.

How share prices are determined

Share prices are determined according to the economic laws of supply and demand. In general, if there are more buyers than sellers, the price will rise, whereas if there are more sellers than buyers, the price will fall. When buyers and sellers compete in the market, they consider not just past performance but also future expectations. Indeed it's almost always the case that the market looks forward more than it looks backward. It's similar to driving a motorcar; you look forward most of the time but occasionally glance at the rear vision mirror to see what's behind you. That's really how the market works. However, this analogy shouldn't be carried too far because when you drive a car you can see what's ahead, but in the case of the sharemarket what's ahead isn't known and can only be predicted. Of course, that introduces an element of uncertainty (probability) into the share pricing equation.

Tip

The market prices shares more on future expectations (probability) than on past performance (certainty).

Blue sky potential

There are many listed companies whose shares trade for prices ranging from cents to dollars that fit into one or more of the following categories:

⇨ The company doesn't yet have a saleable product.

⇨ The company is making a loss.

⇨ The company has never made a profit.

You'll find examples of these types of companies among:

⇨ mineral and oil exploration companies

⇨ biotechnology or medical companies researching or developing a new vaccine or medical treatment

⇨ industrial innovation companies developing a new product

⇨ computer technology companies developing software or new computer hardware.

And the list goes on ...

Shares in these types of companies are priced by the market according to what is known as 'blue sky potential'. The market factors expected future profitability into the share price, and so companies not currently making a profit may still have a high price if the market anticipates that future profitability may occur.

Tip

It's risky to buy shares in a company whose shares are priced on blue sky potential.

Profiting from shares

As I've said, it's very difficult (impossible?) to consistently beat the market. You might think that's bad news, but if you're a long-term investor it's really a big ray of sunshine for you. That's because it means that in the long run you can do at least as well as the market by following a few simple principles. In other words, trying to beat the market consistently is a futile exercise and doesn't warrant the time, effort and money many share traders devote to this pursuit. In fact, it's an elusive holy grail. I'm confident that if you follow the principles outlined in this book you will have an excellent chance of avoiding disasters and you'll be able to make good long-term profits from shares.

Tip

You can make good long-term profits with shares if you follow some simple strategies and basic principles.

Contradictory strategies

As I point out in the last chapter of my book *Teach Yourself About Shares*, for almost any strategy that's been proposed as a good one with shares, there's also a contradictory one. And the interesting thing I've discovered is that a strategy may work in certain circumstances whereas in different circumstances the contradictory strategy may work just as well. There are several important conclusions you can draw from this:

⇨ There's no one strategy with shares that works in all circumstances.

⇨ The most important factor is to decide on a strategy and stick to it. Chopping and changing at the spur of the moment and not sticking to your strategy is the cause of most problems in share investing.

Tip

When you've decided on a strategy, stick to it. Give it a fair trial, and change only if the fair trial convinces you that your strategy needs to be adjusted (or abandoned).

Some definitions

I don't want to bore you with definitions, but before moving on I need to explain a few important terms.

Share: A share is a portion of ownership in a business enterprise.

Stock: Stock is the total of all the shares issued by the business. The word 'stock' is also used to mean the business enterprise itself. For example, Woolworths, ANZ Bank and BHP Billiton are all stocks. (The terms stock and share are sometimes used interchangeably.)

Listed stock: A listed stock is one whose shares are listed on a stock exchange and can be freely traded (bought or sold) by anyone.

Parcel: A parcel is simply a bundle of shares.

Portfolio: A portfolio is the total shareholding of an investor.

My disclaimer

Right now, I'd better throw in a disclaimer. I believe the principles and strategies I outline in this book are sound and should produce good returns for long-term investors. However, each investor has different resources and requirements that are unique. For example, one investor may be approaching retirement and keen to expand his or her financial nest egg for the future, whereas another may be starting out with little capital and wanting to make some quick profits with shares.

I'm not a financial adviser and I don't know your situation, so I can't give you any advice as to the best strategies for your particular financial resources and requirements. And of course no-one can predict the future—least of all on the sharemarket where unforseen developments can and do occur. While I believe that the principles and strategies I outline apply in general to most investors, that's not to say they're good for all investors at all times. So I strongly suggest that you very carefully consider the information in this book and decide for yourself whether or not you want to adopt all or some of my suggestions.

Tip

If you obtain factual and reliable information, don't underestimate your ability to make sound decisions based upon it. When investors make unsound decisions it's usually because those decisions are based upon unsound information or gut feelings and not because the investor has insufficient intellectual capacity.

Chapter summary

⇨ While everyone wants to make money on the sharemarket, it's important to put wealth accumulation into perspective and realise that money's not the be all and end all in life.

⇨ You don't need to rely on the expertise of others to make good profits from shares.

⇨ It's very difficult to beat the market over the long term, and if the performance of your share portfolio matches the market, you're doing well.

⇨ The performance of the market is an average performance. In any given year, some shares do better than the market and some do worse.

⇨ The market determines the prices of shares and the market price reflects the true value of those shares at the time.

⇨ A share may outperform the market over some time period, but there's bound to be a correction.

⇨ If a number of shares in your portfolio outperform the market, these shares will tend to compensate for any you might hold that underperform the market.

⇨ It's generally safer to follow the market than to trade against it (contrarian approach).

⇨ A complex approach that requires much time and effort in research and share trading won't necessarily produce better results than a simple approach that doesn't require a lot of time and effort.

⇨ Unless you're a very experienced investor, it's best to stick to Australian shares that are listed on the Australian Securities Exchange (ASX).

⇨ Shares whose prices are based on blue sky potential are more risky and best avoided.

⇨ The key to success with share investing is sticking to the strategy you decide to adopt and not deviating from it without a very good reason for doing so.

chapter 2

Profiting from shares

In this chapter I'll describe how you can profit with shares and some of the factors you need to consider in order to maximise your profitability. I'll also outline the taxation implications that can affect your profitability and influence your decisions.

There are two ways (and only two) that you can make a profit from shares. They are:

⇨ capital gains

⇨ dividends.

Profiting from capital gains

You make a capital gain when you sell shares for a higher price than you paid for them. When you buy or sell shares this is known as trading, and those who do it frequently are known as traders. In most cases you trade shares using an agent known as a stockbroker. Naturally a stockbroker charges a fee for service (called brokerage) and that fee will reduce the amount of profit you make on the trade.

When you sell shares for a profit you make a real capital gain. If the shares go up in price after you buy them and you keep holding but don't sell, you're making a theoretical capital gain, known as a 'paper' or 'unrealised' capital gain.

Tip

It's very difficult to be successful in the long term if you frequently trade shares. It's much easier to be successful investing for the long term and trading infrequently.

Example 1

You buy 1000 shares for $1.00 each and sell them for $1.50 each, and the brokerage per trade is $30.

What's your net capital gain?

Solution

You make a capital gain of 50¢ per share, so for 1000 shares you make a total capital gain of $500. Since the brokerage charge is $30 per trade, on the combined buy and sell trades the total brokerage is $60 and your net capital gain is **$440**.

Tip

The brokerage charge cuts into your profit, so the lower the charge the higher your profit from the trade. The best way of reducing the brokerage charge is to trade using the internet, because internet-based brokers charge a lower fee. I'll discuss this in greater detail later in the book.

But let's face it, share investing doesn't always result in a capital gain. Sometimes you buy shares and sell them for less than what you paid for them. In such cases you make a capital loss that's a real loss. You make a paper (unrealised) loss if you don't sell but continue to hold.

Tip

Brokers charge the same fee for selling regardless of the outcome of the trade.

Example 2

You buy 1000 shares for $1.00 and sell them for 50¢ and the brokerage per trade is $30. What's your total capital loss?

Solution

You make a capital loss of 50¢ per share, so for 1000 shares you make a capital loss of $500 on the trade. On the combined buy and sell trades the total brokerage is $60, so your total capital loss is **$560**.

Tip

Brokerage reduces *your profit with a successful trade* and increases *your loss with an unsuccessful one.*

Tax on capital gains

If you make a net capital gain from share trading it's considered as taxable income and must be declared in your taxation return for the financial year in which the sell trade occurred. For example, if you sell prior to 30 June, the capital gain must be included in that financial year's tax return, regardless of when you bought the shares. Brokerage is an allowable deduction that you take into consideration when calculating net capital gain (or loss) from each trade. A net capital gain is taxed in the same way as any other income, with one exception. If you've held the shares for one year or longer, only *half* the capital gain is considered as taxable income. If you make a net capital loss in any financial year, you can't write the loss off against other income in that year. All you can do is carry the loss forward until such time that you make a capital gain, and then you can write the loss off against the gain.

Unless share trading is your primary source of income, you don't need to declare paper capital gains as these aren't considered to be income until you actually sell.

Tip

If you've bought some shares that you're thinking of selling for a profit and you've held them for a little less than one year, it may pay to hang on to them until you've held them for a year before you sell because of the tax saving.

Tax on combined trades

When in any financial year you sell some shares for a profit and some for a loss, you can write total capital losses off against total net gains to calculate your taxable income. If you've held the shares you sold for a profit for a year or more, you can then apply the 50% discount.

Example 3

In a tax year, you sell some shares for a net profit of $860. In the same year, you sell some shares for a total loss of $240. Work out your taxable income from share trading if:

a) you've held the profitable shares for less than one year

b) you've held the profitable shares for more than one year.

Solution

a) You've held the profitable shares for less than one year, so your taxable income is:

$$860 - 240 = \textbf{\$620}$$

b) You've held your profitable shares for more than one year, so your taxable income is:

$$(860 - 240) \div 2 = \textbf{\$310}$$

In case b) you can't work it out this way (as much as you might like to):

860 ÷ 2 − 240 = $190

Profiting from dividends

Many companies pay a dividend on the shares they issue. The dividend is a payment to shareholders who own the shares before a certain cut-off date, known as the ex-dividend date. Dividends are usually paid twice a year on dates declared by the company directors. The first dividend in the company's financial year is known as the interim dividend and the second dividend is known as the final dividend. The total dividend for the year is the sum of the two. The final dividend is usually somewhat greater than the interim dividend but that's by no means always the case.

You profit from dividends because they're a cash payment that you'll receive by cheque or as a direct deposit in your nominated bank account. They're very much like an interest payment on capital invested.

Tip

The beauty of dividends is that if you hold the shares over the long term, you'll continue to receive the dividend as a regular payment. So if you're a long-term shareholder, the money will roll in every six months as regular income without you needing to do anything at all.

Not all financial managers or advisers agree that dividends are good for shareholders. Some argue that shareholders are better off if the company retains all profit and reinvests it back into the business. My view is that the shareholders are the owners of the business, and what's the point of owning a business if you don't receive a share of the income made by it? After all, the board of directors and senior executives of the business all help themselves to a healthy slice of the company's income, so why shouldn't the shareholders be given some? I'll discuss this issue in greater detail in later chapters.

Ex-dividend date

If you buy shares at any time before the ex-dividend date, you'll receive the current dividend. If you buy them on the ex-dividend date or later, you'll miss out on that dividend.

Don't confuse the ex-dividend date with the date the dividend is declared, as they're not the same. The date the dividend is declared is always before the ex-dividend date and is the date when the company directors announce the dividend. The date the dividend is actually paid out is usually a month or two after the ex-dividend date, and you'll receive that dividend even if you've sold the shares after the ex-dividend date.

Tip

Unfortunately, there's no easy way of determining the ex-dividend date in advance. Usually the ex-dividend date doesn't vary much from year to year. So if last year the ex-dividend date was 26 August, then it's a good chance that this year the ex-dividend date will also be around 26 August.

Dividend per share

The dividend is almost always quoted in cents per share and shown in share listings as dividend per share (DPS). The total amount of dividend you'll receive is the DPS multiplied by the number of eligible shares you hold.

Example 4

You're a long-term holder of 1000 shares in a company that declares an interim dividend of 4¢ per share and final dividend of 5¢ per share. What dividend will you receive for the whole financial year?

Solution

Your total dividend is:

4¢ + 5¢ = 9¢ per share

Since you hold 1000 shares, your dividend for the year will be: 9000¢ = **$90**

Payout ratio

Dividends are a proportion of the company profits that's paid out to shareholders. The proportion of the company profits that each shareholder receives is known as the payout ratio. It's usually expressed as a decimal figure or as a percentage. So if the payout ratio is 0.6 or 60%, this means that 60% of the after-tax profit is paid to shareholders.

Yield

The yield is the annual dividend per share divided by the share price and is shown as a percentage. It's equivalent to the percentage interest on the current value of the shares.

Yield is based on the current price of the shares, not what you paid for them when you purchased them.

Example 5

You own some shares that are currently trading for $2.00 each and the annual dividend per share is 9¢. What is the yield?

Solution

The dividend of 9¢ per share expressed in dollars is $0.09:

The yield is: $0.09 \div 2 = 0.045$
To convert to a percentage, multiply by 100
Therefore the yield = **4.5%**

The dividend per share changes only every six months as the latest interim and final dividends are declared. However, the share price changes with each trade on the market.

Price fluctuations affect the yield as follows:

⇨ If the share price rises, the yield reduces.

⇨ If the share price falls, the yield increases.

Tip

A short-cut way of calculating the yield is to divide the dividend in cents by the share price in dollars. This automatically gives the yield as a percentage.

So in the above example, $9 \div 2 = 4.5\%$ (easy isn't it?).

In most share listings the yield is shown, so you won't need to do the calculation. However, it's not always shown (particularly for mining shares). In any case it's a good idea to be able to calculate it yourself so as to get a better understanding of yield.

Significance of yield

Dividends are great for long-term investors because they're money that rolls in every six months and this provides a steady income. Yield is significant because it gives you a yardstick by which you can compare different shares on the basis of the amount of income you'll receive as a proportion of the amount of capital invested. It also allows you to rate shares as a long-term investment compared to other types of investment that provide interest income, such as term deposits or bonds.

Tip

An easy way you can compare dividends and yields with listed companies is from share listings in the financial pages of most newspapers. You'll find a column headed 'yield' and you need only look down this column. If there's no yield shown, it means that no dividend was paid. When you look at these listings you'll discover that, contrary to what you might expect, the majority of listed companies don't pay dividends. In particular, most mining companies don't pay dividends.

Franking

Australian companies are required to pay tax on their profits. If the company pays a dividend, it often comes out of the after-tax profits. So when you receive a dividend paid from company profit that's already been taxed by the Australian Taxation Office (ATO), you'll receive a tax credit for the tax the company has already paid on its profit. The amount of tax credit you'll receive is called the franking credit or imputation credit. If the company has paid full tax on its profits, the dividend is fully franked, but if no tax has been paid the dividend is unfranked. For in-between levels of taxation, the dividend will be partly franked.

When you submit your tax return, you'll receive the tax credit as a dollar rebate (or offset) after the tax on your taxable income is calculated. If you don't need to pay Australian tax, you can still receive the franking credit as a dollar deposit by lodging a tax return.

Some companies with shares listed on the ASX don't pay Australian tax on some or all of their profits if they're registered overseas or have overseas affiliates.

Tip

If you don't need to submit a tax return (for example, if your taxable income is below the tax-free threshold) but have some franking credits, it may pay to still submit a tax return to obtain the tax credit as a payment from the ATO.

Company tax rates

The tax rate for companies at the time of writing is 30% of their profit (or earnings). This means that if your personal income is such that you're in the 30% tax bracket, any fully franked dividend you receive is tax-free. If your tax rate is higher than 30%, you pay tax on the dividend only on the difference between your tax rate and 30%.

Grossing dividends

Regardless of your tax situation, a fully franked dividend is much better for you than an unfranked one. You can calculate how much better it is using a figure known as the grossing-up factor. If the franked dividend is multiplied by the grossing-up factor, the result is the equivalent unfranked dividend.

For a fully franked dividend the grossing-up factor is 1.429, but 1.43 is close enough.

T?p

To find out the grossing-up factor for partly franked dividends, please refer to my book Teach Yourself About Shares *(table 4.3).*

Example 6

What's a better yield for you, 6% fully franked or 8% unfranked?

Solution

Using the grossing-up factor of 1.43, the equivalent unfranked yield of the 6% fully franked yield is:

$$1.43 \times 6 = 8.58\%$$

Therefore because of the value of the imputation credits, a fully franked yield of 6% is equivalent to an 8.58% unfranked yield. Therefore the answer to the question is that a **6% fully franked yield is better** for you than an 8% unfranked yield.

Tax minimisation

Any tax paid on profits reduces your return on the capital invested, so it's important to try to minimise (or eliminate) tax on profits. You can eliminate capital gains tax by not selling and simply holding on to your shares. You can eliminate tax on dividends if they're fully franked and your marginal tax rate is the same as or less than the company tax rate (30%). If you're on a higher marginal tax rate than 30%, you can't avoid paying tax on dividends at a rate equal to the difference between your marginal tax rate and the company tax rate, unless you purchased the shares in the name of a family member who is at a lower (or zero) tax rate.

Tip

Schemes for which the sole purpose is to reduce tax are, in general, illegal. However, there are legitimate ways of reducing tax and it may be worthwhile seeking advice from an accountant to investigate if there are tax-saving strategies you can employ, such as setting up a self managed superannuation fund (SMSF) or a trust for your shares.

Obtaining the data

How do you get the information you need to work out capital gains and dividends and to know if the dividend is franked, unfranked or partly franked? A quick and easy way of obtaining this data is from the financial pages of newspapers that print share listings showing share prices and dividend yields. As an example I've used the financial pages in *The Sydney Morning Herald* for industrial shares. The format is as shown in table 2.1 (overleaf).

This share listing is for industrial shares. The listing of mining shares in *The Sydney Morning Herald* is a little different because most mining shares don't pay a dividend. To find out the dividend for mining shares, you'll need to conduct research on the internet or use a specialist financial publication such as the *Financial Review* or the *Financial Review Smart Investor* magazine (published monthly and available at newsagents).

This listing was current at the time of writing, and of course won't be up to date at the time you're reading this book.

Table 2.1: typical extract from a share listing

Company	Last sale	+ or −	No. sold 100s	Closing quotes Buy	Closing quotes Sell	Div yld %	PE ratio	52 week High	52 week Low
CBA	58.14	+21	26,621	58.12	58.14	4.04f	17.6	58.65	33.95
CBD Energy	.13		5,180	.13	.135			.195	.031
CFS Retail	1.87	+1.5	70,529	.1.86	1.865	6.7		2.12	1.42
Computershr	12.64	+5	10,941	12.64	12.65	1.98p	22.2	12.90	8.31

I'll now explain the columns in this listing, from left to right:

⇨ Company: the name of the company (often abbreviated); for example, CBA stands for Commonwealth Bank of Australia.

⇨ Last sale: the last sale price in dollars (at the close of trade the previous day).

⇨ + or − : the price move in cents on the previous day compared to the close the day before, with + meaning a price rise and − meaning a price fall.

⇨ No. sold: the number of shares traded on the previous day in hundreds.

⇨ Closing quotes: the buyers' closest bid and the sellers' closest offer at the close of trade.

⇨ Dividend yield: the dividend yield as a percentage of the closing price. The small letter after the dividend tells you if the dividend is fully franked (f) or partly franked (p). If no letter appears, the dividend is unfranked. If no dividend is shown, this means no dividend was paid in the previous financial year. You can see the dividends in this example are as follows:

  ▫ CBA = 4.04% fully franked

  ▫ CBD Energy = no dividend

  ▫ CFS Retail = 6.7% unfranked

  ▫ Computershare = 1.98% partly franked.

⇨ PE ratio: the price to earnings ratio (I'll discuss this in detail in later chapters).

⇨ 52-week high/low: the highest and lowest closing prices of the shares in the previous 52 weeks.

Chapter summary

⇨ You can make profits from shares in two ways: from capital gains and dividends.

⇨ Capital gains are made when you sell shares for a higher price than you paid for them. If you don't sell the shares but hold them, your capital gain is a theoretical (or paper) gain and not an actual gain (dollars in the bank).

⇨ Actual capital gains are income and are taxed accordingly in the taxation year that the sale took place. If you hold shares for longer than a year, only half the gain is taxable income.

⇨ Dividends are a proportion of company profits paid to investors holding shares prior to a certain date known as the ex-dividend date.

⇨ Dividends are usually paid twice a year; the first dividend is known as the interim dividend and the second one is called the final dividend.

⇨ Not all listed companies pay a dividend. In particular, mining companies and new venture companies seldom pay a dividend.

⇨ Dividends are income and are taxed accordingly. However, if the company has paid Australian tax on its profits, the dividend is franked and the shareholder will receive a tax credit for the tax already paid by the company.

⇨ If the shares are fully franked, there is a 30% tax credit on the dividend so a shareholder on a tax rate of 30% receives the dividend tax-free.

⇨ The yield is the total annual dividend divided by the share price (expressed as a percentage) and is equivalent to interest on the current value of the shares.

⇨ To compare fully franked and unfranked yields, multiply a fully franked yield by the grossing-up factor to get the equivalent unfranked dividend. This is called the grossed-up yield.

⇨ For fully franked dividends the grossing-up factor is 1.43. For partly franked dividends the grossing-up factor will vary between 1.00 and 1.43, depending on the level of franking.

⇨ Tax reduces your investment income and rate of return, so you need to adopt strategies to minimise your tax obligations.

⇨ An easy way of finding out dividends is from the financial listings in a newspaper where there's a column headed 'Yield' or 'Dividend per share (DPS)'.

chapter 3

The power of compounding

In this chapter I discuss the power of compounding, and lay the groundwork for a reliable method that you can use for long-term wealth accumulation with shares.

Compounding returns

Compounding kicks in when you make a profit on an investment and you reinvest that profit. In the case of an investment in an interest-bearing account, this is known as compound interest. On the other hand, if you don't reinvest your profits this is known as simple interest.

Tip

Compounding is very important and really kicks in over the long term. If you're trying to make a short-term gain (for example, by short-term share trading), you don't need to consider compounding as it's not significant in

*the short term. The longer the term of the investment, the
more benefit you'll derive from compounding.*

Compounding works because by reinvesting your profits
you're adding to your investment capital. If you reinvest
your profits this year, then next year you'll make more profit
because you're getting a return on the capital reinvested in
addition to the capital you originally invested. In effect, next
year you're making a profit on the profit you made this year.

Tip

*To make compounding work, you need to reinvest profits
and not withdraw them. It's a human temptation to want
to spend profits, but if you want to really grow your
wealth over the long term you must resist the impulse to
spend in the short term.*

Example 1

You invest $100000 in a portfolio of shares. Your portfolio
makes a profit of 10% in the first year and you reinvest your
profit (that is, you don't sell any shares to realise the gains).
Calculate the value of your portfolio after the second year
if the portfolio again returns 10%, and work out your total
profit from the investment.

Solution

In the first year, your profit = $10000

Because you reinvest your profit, your portfolio will be worth
$110000 at the end of the year

Next year, your profit is 10% of $110000 = $11000

So at the end of the second year, your portfolio will be worth
$121000

Total profit from the investment = **$21 000**

What if you don't allow the investment to compound? Let's suppose you decide not to reinvest your profit but spend it instead. The difference is shown in example 2.

Example 2

Use the same figures as in example 1, but this time take out your profit after the first year.

Solution

In the first year, your profit = $10 000

You take out the profit of $10 000 by selling some shares and your portfolio will again be worth $100 000 at the end of the year

The next year your profit is 10% of $100 000 = $10 000

At the end of the second year, your portfolio will be worth **$100 000** if you again take out your profit

Total profit from the investment = **$20 000**

You can see from example 1 that by reinvesting profits you've increased the value of your portfolio by $21 000 over just two years. Also you've made an additional $1000 profit in the second year from compounding. The additional profit of $1000 doesn't sound like much as it's only 1% of your invested capital, but in the long term compounding makes a huge difference, as I'll show you shortly.

The effect of inflation

There's another problem that arises with an investment if you don't compound profits. Throughout most nations in the world (including Australia), inflation is a fact of life. Simply put, inflation is the overall increase in the price of goods and services as time passes, and the inflation rate is this change expressed as a percentage over a one-year period. The causes of inflation involve rather complex economics but the simple explanation is that it's very difficult (if not impossible) for a nation to balance its finances exactly and governments prefer modest inflation to the alternative of deflation (decreases in prices). In Australia, government policy for some years has been to try to keep inflation to about 3% or lower.

Money of itself has almost no intrinsic value, and $100 in your wallet has value only because you can buy $100 worth of goods or services with it. If you keep the $100 in your wallet for a year and the inflation rate is 3%, then next year if you do spend the $100 you can buy only about $97 worth of goods or services with it. In other words, you've lost around $3 in a year just by holding cash that hasn't earned a profit and kept up with inflation.

Tip

A good way of thinking about the eroding effect of inflation is to consider that when your money isn't invested in some way and earning a return, your money is 'taking a holiday'.

The growth rate of an investment after inflation is taken into account is known as the 'inflation-adjusted return', 'real rate of return' or 'rate of return in real terms'.

Tip

To maintain the value of any investment, you must earn and reinvest profits at least at the same rate as inflation. If the inflation rate is 3%, this means that you must make an after-tax profit of at least 3% on your investment capital and reinvest it each year to ensure that your real wealth doesn't decrease.

What happens if I make a loss?

So far, I've assumed that your investment produces a profit. What about if you don't make a profit on the investment, so you have no profit to reinvest? Hopefully if you adopt the principles and strategies outlined in this book that situation should be fairly rare, but in some years it can happen and your shares might show zero growth or decline. In that case, don't panic; remember that the bad times won't last forever and you should be able to more than make up losses in one or two years by gains in following years. What's important is the average return on a long-term investment, not the profit or loss in any one or two years.

Tip

It's often the case that a bad year with shares will be followed by an excellent one. It's very important to realise this and not to panic should the market turn down. Indeed, market downturns can be opportunities to make great profits because they allow you to buy good shares at bargain prices.

Compounding capital gains

You can obtain the benefit of compounding capital gains without doing anything at all. If you invest long term and resist the temptation to spend any capital gains, compounding kicks in automatically for you, and as share prices increase your investment capital increases. This is because compounding is based on a percentage increase in value and not a fixed amount of dollars. So as the value of your portfolio increases, the same percentage return on it produces an ever-increasing profit.

Tip

Capital gains compound with shares if you hold them long term and their prices increase, and you don't sell.

Compounding dividends

As well as compounding your capital gains, you can compound dividends. If there's a dividend reinvestment plan (DRP) available, you can do this automatically by joining the plan. Then your dividends will be converted into shares and you need take no further action.

Not all listed companies offer a DRP; many prefer to pay dividends in cash rather than shares. In such cases, to compound dividends you need to put the dividend cash aside in an investment account and buy more shares when you've accumulated enough cash in the account to make a share purchase worthwhile.

There's no difference in the tax treatment of dividends taken as cash or reinvested by way of a DRP. The dividends need to be included in exactly the same way in a tax return. To find out which companies have a DRP, you need to delve further. I'll show you how to do so in later chapters.

Tip

If a DRP is available, it can be a good idea to join it.

Compounding is reliable

In chapter 1, I discussed the idea of beating the market and obtaining superior returns. Rather like the alchemists of old who tried to turn lead into gold, traders have been trying to develop a 'get rich quick' share trading system that works all the time. The reality is that no-one has yet devised one. Even the power of computers doesn't help because share prices are determined by people, and people have moods and emotions that don't follow a constant pattern and are unpredictable. That's the bad news; the good news is that compounding is a mathematical principle that never fails because mathematical laws are infallible and not subject to the vagaries of human nature. Compounding is far and away the most reliable method you can use to build your wealth over an extended time frame.

Tip

Don't be tempted to spend a great deal of money on a computer system or method that claims to produce fantastic profits with shares. If you devised such a system, would you sell it to anyone else? Compounding capital gains and dividends is a proven and reliable long-term investment strategy that doesn't require any costly whiz-bang computer programs or expert advice.

Rule of 72

You can calculate the effect of compounding by using a mathematical formula known as the compound interest formula. I quote this formula in my book *Teach Yourself About Shares*, and I also provide a compound interest table that gives compound factors for various annual growth values and time periods. However, there's also a simple rule known as the Rule of 72 that provides a good guide to the effect of compounding. It's not precise, but it gives answers that are generally accurate enough.

The Rule of 72 is as follows:

The number of years to double in value = 72 ÷ Annual growth rate

Example 3

Use the Rule of 72 to work out how long it will take for prices to double if inflation averages 3% per year.

Solution

72 ÷ 3 = 24

Therefore it will take **24 years** for prices to double.

Twenty-four years seems like a long time doesn't it, but when you consider that nowadays average life expectancy is more than 72 years, this means that prices will double more than three times in an average lifetime. There'll be an eightfold increase in prices over this period of time. So a property worth, say, $500000 today would be worth $4000000 in 72 years if the price simply keeps up with inflation. Put another way, something you buy for $1.00 today will cost $8.00 in 72 years.

Target returns

The Rule of 72 implies that if you can average a 7.2% return on an investment, you will double the value of your invested capital in 10 years. This means that if you invest $10000 today, your investment will be worth $20000 after 10 years, and after 20 years it will double again and your investment will be worth $40000. Better still, if you can average a 10% return your investment will double in value in 7.2 years, and double in value again in another 7.2 years. So after 14.4 years, $10000 will grow to $40000.

These figures provide a good target or benchmark that you can aim for when looking at a long-term investment. Of course, if you can achieve a higher rate of return, then well and good. For example, if you can average a 14.4% return on your investment, it will double in value in only five years! While that sounds fantastic, and may well be achievable with your shares, I don't recommend you plan for such a high rate of return over the long term.

Tip

For long-term investing, a 10% average return is very satisfactory. Of course the higher the rate of return the better, but you don't need to get a really high rate of return to grow your investment capital over the long term. If you stay above the inflation rate, you will ensure that your real wealth increases.

Chapter summary

⇨ There's no magic system for beating the sharemarket.

⇨ There's a mathematical principle that's infallible and it's known as compounding. It's the most reliable way to grow your wealth over the long term with shares (or any investment for that matter).

⇨ Compounding will grow your wealth over the long term, but it's of little help in the short term.

⇨ You obtain the benefit of compounding by reinvesting your profits and not spending them.

⇨ Compounding requires discipline to avoid the temptation of spending your profits now.

⇨ For long-term investing, a loss in any one or two years is not significant, provided that there's average profitability over the long term.

⇨ You automatically compound capital gains when you simply hold on to your shares and don't sell them.

⇨ You can automatically compound dividends by joining a dividend reinvestment plan, but not all companies that pay dividends provide this facility.

⇨ If there's no DRP, you can still compound dividends if you add them to your investment capital and buy more shares with them (after you've accumulated enough money to make it worthwhile).

⇨ The Rule of 72 provides an easy way of working out how long it will take to double the value of your investment for different rates of return.

⇨ A good benchmark for long-term investing is an average growth rate of 10%. Then your investment will double in value after 7.2 years.

⇨ The higher the rate of return the faster your investment will grow, but it's not easy to average a really high rate of return over the long term.

⇨ Inflation erodes the value of any investment because it reduces the purchasing power of money.

⇨ Money that isn't invested in some way and earning a profit is 'taking a holiday'. In fact, it's falling in real value (purchasing power).

⇨ In order to grow your real wealth, you need to obtain a rate of return after tax that's higher than the inflation rate.

chapter 4

Investing in Australian shares

In this chapter I'll consider the outlook for the Australian economy and the reasons why investing in Australian shares is one of the best ways of making profits and growing your wealth.

Why invest in Australian shares?

When I ceased full-time employment in the year 2000, I wanted to invest some of my funds in allocated pensions to obtain tax-free income for future years. I consulted a well-recognised firm of investment advisers and I was advised to allocate a fair proportion of my available capital to global (or international) shares, particularly the US market. The reasons for doing so seemed logical, including the fact that US shares had performed extremely well for some years prior to 2000. The Australian market was less than 2% of the world market (as measured by the value of capital invested), and indeed the shares in some US companies such as Microsoft were worth more than the total value of all shares in the Australian market! I was told I had a wonderful opportunity to get with the strength and invest in multinational corporations such as Microsoft, IBM, Kentucky Fried, McDonald's and General Motors.

The advice seemed good, so I allocated a fair chunk of my investment capital to global shares. And from that day to this, the global shares segment of my allocated pensions has underperformed the Australian shares segment and never caught up! For example, table 4.1 shows a typical allocated pension report I received at the end of April 2010. (This report included the downturn due to the global financial crisis in 2008–09.)

Table 4.1: share performance at the end of April 2010

	One-year performance	Performance since inception
Australian shares option	43.5%	10.7%
Global shares option	9.18%	–3.0%

These statistics speak for themselves. So much for getting with global sharemarket strength!

Difficulties with global shares

Apart from underperformance, some other problems that arise with investing in corporations outside Australia are:

⇨ It's much more difficult to get up-to-date information and to keep abreast of developments.

⇨ There's an additional risk due to exchange rate fluctuations that can go against you. So a profit in an overseas currency can end up as a loss when converted to Australian dollars.

⇨ Most brokers charge a higher brokerage fee if you want to trade international shares.

⇨ Dividends are unlikely to carry any Australian franking credits.

Tip

For your share portfolio, invest only in listed Australian shares.

Positives for the Australian economy and for Australian shares

I'll now consider some of the positives for the Australian economy and for Australian shares.

Growing population

Australia's population has been expanding steadily over many decades, and the rate of population growth is now higher than it was in the boom decade of the 1960s. This population growth is a result of high rates of childbirth and immigration (mainly skilled workers and their families). In addition, life expectancies are also increasing—people are living longer.

Australia's expanding population is good for business and provides continuing profit growth opportunities for Australian companies. Increased population affects company profitability in the following way:

Increasing population ➔ Increasing demand ➔ Increasing sales ➔ Increasing profits

As the population increases, there's increasing demand for consumer goods and services, and also for housing and construction and the entire infrastructure needed to service this increased population.

Is Australia's population growth likely to slow in the foreseeable future? Most economists believe that Australia can support a much higher population than we currently have. Information released by the Rudd Government in October

2009 revealed that Australia's population had grown by 2.1% in the year to date, which was among the highest population growths in the developed world. Further, the government projected that Australia's population would increase from the current level of 21.5 million to 35 million in another 30 or 40 years. So it seems reasonable to assume that Australia's population will continue to grow in the foreseeable future.

All this bodes well for the Australian economy and for Australian business. When company profits increase, share-holders benefit because share prices and dividends increase in proportion to profitability.

Tip

Australia's population seems set to increase steadily in the coming decades, and this provides an inbuilt growth factor for Australian businesses and the Australian sharemarket.

High living standard

The standard of living in Australia is high and this is reflected in our thriving economy, with high demand for goods and services. And high demand for goods and services is good for Australian businesses that provide the goods and services consumers require to support their standard of living. In addition, Australia has a well-structured and widespread education and training system that provides opportunities for a high standard of education for all Australians. A spin-off benefit of this is that many other countries are sending students to study in Australia, and this provides a valuable source of overseas income that benefits all Australians.

Profit reinvestment

It's a well-accepted principle of business that a proportion of company profits should be retained and reinvested in the business. Australian companies that make a profit almost always follow this principle and distribute only a proportion of their earnings to shareholders in the form of dividends. The rest of the profit is retained in the business and used for purposes such as debt reduction, expansion, upgrading of assets such as plant and facilities, and research and development.

How does this affect shareholders? In the discussion of compounding in chapter 2, I pointed out that compounding kicks in for you when you reinvest your profits from an investment. Over an extended time period, the increase in value compounds at an ever-growing rate. The same effect takes place in business, and by reinvesting profits companies grow in value at an ever-increasing rate. As the value of a company increases, earnings should increase in proportion. That's to say, the more a company is worth, the more profit it should make in the future, provided that the reinvested profit is used to improve the business. An increase in company value and profits benefits shareholders and will be reflected in a steady growth in dividends and share values.

Tip

A profitable company is usually a sound long-term investment because a proportion of the earnings will be reinvested into the company to increase its future value and profitability.

Improving technology

Australian companies usually embrace new technology in order to improve efficiency and productivity and to maintain their operations at a best practice standard. Consider the changes that have taken place in the banking industry, where ATMs and computerisation have reduced costs and improved productivity. Other electronic developments, including bar coding and touch-screen checkouts, have also transformed the retail sector, particularly for large retail outlets and petrol stations. Automated warehouses and storage depots, robotics, computer-aided drafting and finite element analysis are some further examples of new technology that Australian companies are embracing to improve productivity and quality.

New technology requires capital investment, but it should more than pay for itself in higher productivity (after a certain period of time, called the payback period). Higher productivity results in higher profitability and return on capital, and is good news for investors.

Tip

There seems to be no foreseeable end to the march of technology. Australian companies that embrace this new technology to enhance quality and productivity should continue to grow their profits and returns to shareholders.

Rationalisation, mergers and takeovers

Rationalisation, mergers and takeovers are other ways for businesses to become more productive. This is generally good for shareholders because better productivity results in higher profits.

Companies can rationalise their operations by concentrating on core competencies and divesting themselves of aspects of their business where they're not at the forefront of best practice. If there's a major split in operations so as to form two companies out of one, this is known — naturally enough — as a split. A good example is when BHP split the resources side of the business from the steel-making side, so now there are two companies operating as separate entities, namely BHP Billiton and Bluescope Steel.

Mergers occur when companies competing in the same industry combine their separate operations into one. A good example is when Adelaide and Bendigo banks combined their operations to form the Bendigo and Adelaide Bank.

Takeovers are very similar to mergers except that the takeover company (predator) remains dominant. They may be friendly or hostile: a friendly takeover is one that's agreed to by the boards of directors of both companies, whereas a hostile takeover is one that's generally opposed by the company being taken over. In Australia there have been many instances in the banking industry where regional banks and finance companies were taken over by one of the big four; for example, Colonial Bank, Rural Bank, Bank of Melbourne, Bank of New South Wales and St George Bank were all taken over. In the retail industry, Dick Smith Electronics and Tandy were taken over by Woolworths and Coles was taken over by Wesfarmers.

Takeovers and mergers reduce competition and reduce costs by creating economies of scale. Economies of scale result from spreading fixed costs over a larger output, so there's a lower cost per unit produced. In addition, larger companies have more sway with suppliers and can negotiate lower purchase prices. However, because takeovers and mergers reduce competition, they may be opposed by the federal government who wants to ensure continuing healthy competition in Australian business in the best interests of consumers, so major takeovers and mergers may require government approval.

Tip

If there's a takeover in the offing, the shares of the company being taken over will usually increase because the predator needs to offer a good price to get shareholder and board approval. The shares in the predator may temporarily fall if the market considers that the price paid was too high.

Hedge against inflation

Australian shares provide an inbuilt hedge against inflation, because when prices rise asset values and profits also rise in proportion and consequently share prices rise in proportion.

So as a shareholder, you're fairly well assured that you won't lose the real value of your investment as prices increase with inflation. That wouldn't be the case if your money were invested in a bank account or term deposit where inflation eats away at the real value of your invested capital.

Tip

Shares in sound Australian businesses provide an inbuilt inflation hedge.

Stable and peaceful economy

Many countries experience internal strife or are in conflict with their neighbours over land allocation or ethnic, cultural or religious differences. Terrorism and instability of government often results in bloodshed and major property damage and, needless to say, this type of instability and conflict isn't good for an economy. Investors are naturally reluctant to invest in such countries because of the risks involved. Internally, valuable resources are diverted away from worthwhile projects such as infrastructure development and education in order to fund weapons, provide medical assistance to injured people and to rebuild homes, businesses and other buildings damaged or destroyed in the conflict.

Australia is one of the most peaceful nations in the world with very little terrorism, civil conflict, war or governmental instability. This makes Australia a low-risk investment haven and also means that valuable and scarce resources aren't wasted on external or internal wars and conflicts.

Tip

Lack of conflict and strife both internally and externally helps to ensure a sound Australian economy.

Strong free-enterprise economy

Australia is a free-enterprise economy; that's to say a capitalistic rather than a socialistic one. There's minimum government intervention in business, and private enterprise is encouraged. Indeed, the federal, state and territory governments have, over the years, been divesting themselves of ownership in business enterprises by selling them or converting them to public companies and thereby reinforcing our free-enterprise economy.

Australian governments at all levels continue to spend on infrastructure and other developments that provide a stimulus for Australian industry. Australia has one of the strongest economies with one of the lowest unemployment rates of developed countries. In this economic climate, well-run businesses can flourish with the potential for continuing good profitability.

Sound economic management

Although there have been some missteps in the past, Australia has a history of generally sound and responsible economic management. Our governments are democratically elected and there's been little corruption. The 2008–09 financial tsunami that affected all world economies was not of Australia's doing but we suffered the backwash caused by unsound mortgage lending practices from large institutions in the US. However, our government took prompt action to prevent a recession, and as a result we were one of the few nations in the world to avoid recession and recover relatively unscathed. Indeed, Australia was the only country out of 32 advanced world economies to record positive economic growth in the financial year 2008–09.

Even though our government strongly supports free enterprise, there are still effective controls in place to ensure a strong banking and financial regulatory system with minimum corruption and a fair go for both shareholders and consumers. There's an extensive body of corporations law that's administered by the Australian Securities & Investments Commission (ASIC), which investigates alleged fraud and prosecutes when necessary. In addition, shareholders obtain further protection because all listed companies must comply with the ASX listing rules and regulations.

Tip

Australia has an effective banking and financial regulatory system. Shareholders in Australian businesses are protected by a vast body of corporate regulation aimed at preventing corruption. However, no amount of financial control can completely eradicate corruption, so you need to exercise a degree of caution, particularly if you invest in smaller, more speculative companies.

Vast resource deposits

Australia is fortunate to have vast deposits of coal, gas, uranium, iron and gold—all of which are important resources for an energy-hungry and developing world. Australian resource companies invest large amounts of capital in resource development and exploration, and this provides a stimulus for other Australian businesses associated with these developments. We also have renewable resources such as wool, wheat and cattle. And of course we're blessed with abundant sunshine and we're at the forefront of solar technology that no doubt will become more and more important as time goes on.

These resources are greater than we require for our own needs, and so can be used to provide export income to help pay for our imports of goods and services that can't be produced economically at home. Strong demand for our resources seems set to continue for some time into the future, particularly as China and India continue along the path of fast economic growth with high demand for many of our resources.

Also, because of our peaceful society, temperate climate, unique flora and fauna, wide open spaces and other attractions that appeal to overseas visitors, we have a thriving tourist industry that provides an important source of overseas income.

Tip

Although there's been much discussion and research aimed at replacing fossil fuels and uranium as energy sources, it's unlikely that the demand for these will reduce significantly for some decades yet.

Track record of Australian shares

Let's now see how the Australian economic positives have been reflected in the sharemarket. A good way of assessing Australian shares as an investment is to look at the performance of the All Ordinaries index (All Ords). This index measures the weighted average share price of the 500 largest companies listed on the ASX. While there are several thousand listed companies, the 500 largest ones represent about 98% of invested dollars and so the All Ords is a very good indicator of Australian market prices as a whole.

Figure 4.1 (overleaf) shows the All Ords from 1980 to the time of writing (October 2009), which is a time period of almost 30 years.

On this chart I've superimposed a long-term trendline, and you can see that despite ups and downs the index trended steadily upward over this long time period. Indeed, if you go back even further in time, you'll find the same upward trend.

Tip

The steady upward march of the All Ords over a long time period has provided excellent capital gains for investors in major Australian shares over the long term.

Figure 4.1: All Ords index over the last 30 years

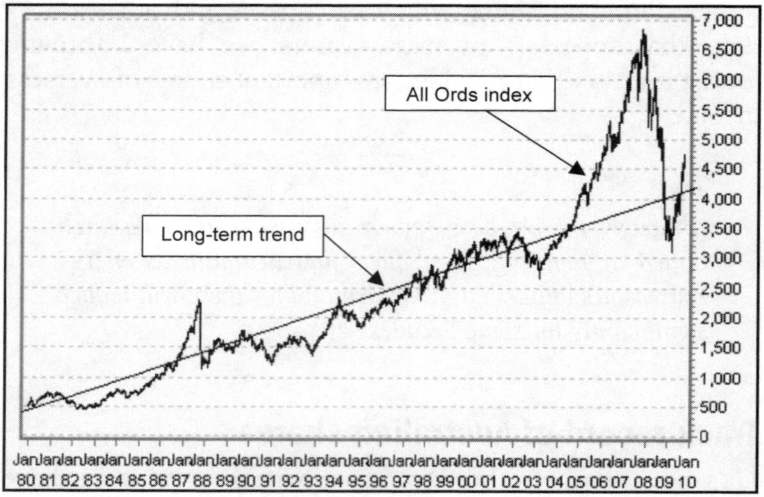

Source: www.CommSec.com.au / Wall St on Demand

What of the future?

In the early 1960s, after graduation, I went overseas and worked for five years in Great Britain and the US, and I also toured around Europe. What I saw convinced me that Australia was not only a great place to live but also a great place for investment. While working in the US I managed to save some money, and on my return to Australia I bought a block of land and also invested in Australian shares. From that day to this, I've had no reason to change my mind about Australia—I'm convinced this is a great country to live in, work in and invest in.

The big question is: can it continue? What does the future hold? It's always dangerous to crystal ball about the future but I'm confident that my children, grandchildren and great grandchildren will all enjoy a good lifestyle in a prosperous Australia. Our population will continue to grow and our natural resources will remain plentiful for many decades to come. Properly managed Australian companies should continue to prosper and their shares should continue to be a good investment in the foreseeable future.

There are some detractors who focus on the negatives for Australia, such as our balance of payments problem and debt obligations of both governments and private individuals. Some believe that the world economy may spiral downward in the future and that this will ripple to Australia (just as the global financial crisis did). You've probably heard the expression, 'when America sneezes the rest of the world gets a cold', and this reinforces the importance of the US economy on the global stage. Naturally, if the global economy gets into trouble again this will affect the Australian economy, but then all nations will be in the same boat and there'll be no safe economic haven anywhere.

Tip

The Australian sharemarket should continue to grow in value into the foreseeable future and provide good profits for investors.

Chapter summary

⇨ It's far easier (and cheaper) to invest in Australian shares than international shares, and Australian shares have performed better over the last decade or so.

⇨ Australia is often described as the 'lucky country' because of our stable government, freedom from conflicts and terrorism, happy-go-lucky and relaxed lifestyle, huge landmass, abundant shoreline and plentiful natural resources.

⇨ Australia's population has been steadily growing and this seems set to continue into the foreseeable future. This population growth provides a stimulus for the Australian economy because it results in increasing demand for goods, services and infrastructure, thereby requiring increasing output of goods and services and providing increasing profits for Australian companies.

⇨ Profitable Australian companies reinvest some of their profits back into the business. This should result in increased value for their shares.

⇨ Shares increase in value because of technology, rationalisation, mergers and takeovers, all of which allow companies to increase productivity and profitability.

⇨ Shares provide an inbuilt hedge against inflation that's not obtained with an interest-bearing investment such as a bank account or term deposit.

⇨ Australia has a history of sound and responsible economic management in a free-enterprise, peaceful and stable economy. This provides the framework for company prosperity and investment growth.

⇨ Shareholders are protected by a vast body of corporations law that's administered by ASIC and by ASX listing rules and regulations.

⇨ Australia's resources will provide an important source of export income for decades to come.

⇨ The All Ords index provides a good measure of about 98% of invested dollars in Australian listed companies.

⇨ The track record of Australia's sharemarket as measured by the All Ords index over past decades includes fluctuations, but the overall trend has been upward over a long period. Over many years Australian shares have proved to be a good investment.

⇨ While the future is never predictable, the outlook for the Australian economy is positive and Australian shares should continue to be a good long-term investment.

chapter 5

Six principles of share investing

In this chapter I describe a relatively hassle-free and low-risk investment strategy that should provide good profitability with shares over the long term. I'll outline the strategy as six principles of investing and I'll expand on these principles in greater detail in later chapters.

The six principles

These principles are as follows:

⇨ Principle 1: Compound your share investment

⇨ Principle 2: Diversify your investment

⇨ Principle 3: Invest in shares with good fundamentals

⇨ Principle 4: Trade at the right price

⇨ Principle 5: Trade at the right time

⇨ Principle 6: Monitor and review regularly

Principle 1: Compound your share investment

As I've already pointed out, if you're really serious about growing your wealth over the long term you need to avoid the temptation of spending profits, whether those profits are in the form of capital gains or dividends. By reinvesting profits you're using the power of compounding for maximum financial benefit. If there's a dividend reinvestment plan available, you can join the plan and dividends will be automatically reinvested for you. If there's no plan available, all you need do is deposit the money in your trading account and when you've accumulated sufficient funds you can buy more shares.

Another benefit of joining a dividend reinvestment plan is that by receiving the dividend in additional shares rather than cash there's less temptation to spend the money. Indeed the only way you can access the money is to sell the extra shares you receive, and unless there's a large number of them it won't be economical for you to do so. So there's an inbuilt incentive to save and accumulate shares.

Tip

A dividend reinvestment plan provides an inbuilt incentive to accumulate shares and benefit from the power of compounding.

Principle 2: Diversify your investment

The principle of diversification is expressed in the well-known adage 'don't put all of your eggs in one basket'. Applied to investing, this principle means that you spread your risk and do not concentrate your wealth in a single asset.

There are many different ways you can invest your money. Spreading your investments across different options provides diversification. Some common options are:

⇨ cash accounts that pay interest, and you can deposit or withdraw as much as you like at any time

⇨ fixed-interest term deposits, where you get a higher rate of interest but your money is locked in for a fixed term and it may be impossible (or costly) to add to or withdraw the invested capital

⇨ gold and precious metals

⇨ artworks, antiques and collectables

⇨ bonds issued by governments (both state and federal)

⇨ direct property, where you become owner or part owner of a block of land, home, home unit or commercial property; many Australians invest directly in property by owning the home in which they reside (principal place of residence)

⇨ indirect property, where you buy units in a fund or trust that invests your money in property

⇨ Australian shares

⇨ international shares

⇨ managed funds, where you buy units in the fund and specialist managers try to maximise the return you will get by investing in various asset groups according to your stated preference

⇨ derivatives such as futures, options, warrants and contracts for difference, where the investment instrument itself has no intrinsic value but derives its value from some other asset class such as commodities, cash or shares.

Each of these different types of investments has advantages and disadvantages that I won't go into, but because you're reading this book I presume you're interested in shares. Even with shares you should diversify and not rely on just one or two stocks. I'll show you how to do this in chapter 7.

Tip

Diversification reduces risk by spreading the risk around.

Principle 3: Invest in shares with good fundamentals

The fundamentals of a company are the basic characteristics of that company that affect investors. As a comparison, think about buying a house that you'd want to live in. Before the property is put on the market the agent will advise the seller to ensure that the 'frilly bits' are right so that the property presents in the best light, with clean and fresh paintwork, neat garden and surrounds and a tidy interior with little clutter and appropriate, strategically placed furniture.

As a buyer you might be influenced by these things, but if you're astute you'll focus more on the fundamentals, such as the location of the property, the land area, the age of the house and the soundness of the construction.

In a similar way, as a share investor you should look beyond surface appearances and consider the fundamentals of a business. In particular, you want to make sure that there are no hidden termites eating away at the structure. Investigation into the fundamentals of companies is a method of analysis known as fundamental analysis. I'll outline the fundamentals you should consider in greater detail in chapter 8, but just to give you the idea they include factors such as how long the business has been in operation, how profitable it has been and what the debt levels are.

Generally speaking, shares with the best fundamentals are high-quality Australian shares. These types of shares are known as 'market leaders' or 'blue-chip' shares. There's no universally agreed definition of what a blue-chip share is but even a novice in the sharemarket will have a fairly good idea of what's meant by this terminology. Blue chips are the most valuable in the casino, and that's where the term comes from, because these shares are usually fairly expensive compared to most others.

Simply put, shares with good fundamentals are less risky and are relatively low maintenance. They're ideal for long-term investors who don't want to trade frequently and spend hours each day studying the market.

Tip

Market leading shares are best for long-term investing.

Principle 4: Trade at the right price

As outlined in Principle 3, investing in shares with good fundamentals is a good long-term strategy. Nevertheless, when you buy (or sell) them you need to do so at the right price. There are many ways of evaluating the 'fairness' of a share price, but the most commonly used are ratios based on price. One such ratio is the PE ratio (I abbreviate to just PE) and another is the PE growth ratio (PEG). I'll show you how to use these ratios in chapter 9 to help you trade at the right price.

At this point you might think, 'Wait a minute, if I want to buy shares how can the price be too low? Surely low-priced shares would be a bargain'. Well no; if you remember in chapter 1 I discussed the efficient market hypothesis, which basically says that investors are fully aware of what's going on and factor everything into the price of shares. So the market price is always right. If a share price seems low, it's most likely low for a good reason and it's probably not a bargain. More likely, the shares will prove to be lemons.

Tip

It's generally risky to buy shares when the price is too high or too low.

Principle 5: Trade at the right time

In addition to ensuring that you're trading at the right price, you need to consider the timing of your trade; that is, when to get in or get out. At this point you might say: 'I can't predict the future, so why worry? It's an each-way bet—after I trade, the share price might rise or it might fall'. You might even quote the common sharemarket saying:

It's not timing the market but time in the market that's important.

Over the long term it's true that time in the market is the most important factor, but let's face it, we all have only one lifetime in which to invest. You don't want to wait for many years to show a capital gain on shares you've bought. Also you don't want to hang on to shares for too long when the price is going down with no sign of recovery.

Assessing the timing of your trades is an area of share-market investing known as technical analysis, and I'll consider it in detail in chapter 10.

Tip

Consider the timing of your share trades in conjunction with price to ensure you're trading at the right time as well as at the right price.

Principle 6: Monitor and review regularly

The basic idea underpinning the investment strategy I am describing is to minimise risks and reduce the time and effort you need to spend on investing. But at the same time you still need to keep an eye on your investment by monitoring and reviewing regularly. You need to consider adjusting the balance of shares in your portfolio if conditions change.

I'll discuss how you can monitor and review your port-folio and what decisions you might need to make in chapters 13 and 14.

Chapter summary

⇨ Use the power of compounding to increase your profitability with shares.

⇨ For maximum long-term gains, reinvest dividends.

⇨ If there's a dividend reinvestment plan, join it. Such plans provide an inbuilt incentive to save and you will obtain the power of compounding with your dividends.

⇨ Diversify your share investments by having a portfolio consisting of a number of different shares.

⇨ Build up a portfolio of high-quality Australian shares.

⇨ Blue-chip shares are market leading shares that are most prized by investors and usually have the highest prices.

⇨ Buy shares when the price is not too high or too low.

⇨ Fundamental analysis helps you evaluate share price value.

⇨ When looking at share price value, two important statistics are the PE ratio and the PEG ratio.

⇨ In addition to trading at the right price, ensure you're trading at the right time.

⇨ Technical analysis helps you to better time your share trades.

⇨ Keep tabs on your share portfolio so you know what's going on.

⇨ Consider changing the mix of your share portfolio should some major change occur.

chapter 6

Building your share portfolio

In this chapter I discuss how you can use compounding to build a substantial share portfolio. I'll demonstrate several options using numerical examples. I'll also discuss planning your share investment and setting realistic goals.

Percentage returns from shares

The All Ords represents the top 500 companies and 98% of all companies in terms of market cap; that is, dollars invested.

At the beginning of 1980 the index had a base value of 500 points. At the beginning of 2008, before the global financial crisis caused a plunge in sharemarkets throughout the world, the All Ords reached a peak of about 6800 points. This is a growth rate of 9.8% over a period of 28 years. At the time of writing (end of October 2009) the index was about 4800 points, and even that value represents a growth rate of 8.4%. This lower figure is the one I'll use in the numerical examples in this chapter.

The All Ords measures prices only and represents the capital gains for share investors in the major Australian companies. On top of the capital gain, most of these companies pay good dividends. Traditionally these have averaged about 4%, although many companies pay higher dividends while with some it's lower. Usually the dividend is fully franked, and then the real value of the 4% yield to an investor is about 5.7%. (At this point you might want to refer back to grossing up of dividends in chapter 2.) If you add the grossed-up yield to the long-term price growth rate of 8.4% in the All Ords, this produces a total investor return of 14.1%. I think you'll agree this is a great rate of return in anyone's language. The Rule of 72 tells us that with this rate of return your invested wealth would double every five years or so!

Tip

When dividend yields and franking are added to capital gains, Australian shares have provided a very good total return for long-term investors that has averaged about 14.1% over the last 30 years or so, despite two major downturns in 1987 and 2008–09.

The effect of taxation

If you're accumulating a share portfolio, capital gains tax doesn't reduce the value of your portfolio because it's payable only when shares are sold. However, dividends must be declared as income in each financial year they're received. I'll show you the effect of taxation on share returns with a numerical example.

Example 1

Let's calculate the total after-tax return for wage earners with and without share portfolios at various levels of income. For these examples I'll use the tax rates current at the time of writing (as shown).

Income ($)	Tax (%)
0 – 6 000	0
6 000 – 35 000	15
35 000 – 80 000	30

I'll assume a share portfolio of value $100000 in shares that pay an average fully franked dividend yield of 4% and where the average capital gain is 8.4%. I'll also assume that the shareholder doesn't sell the shares but holds on to them so the capital gain isn't taxable at this stage. I'll calculate the returns for different taxable income levels with and without shares, as described in the following five scenarios:

⇨ Scenario 1: No taxable income and shares. This would be a common situation for retirees whose main income derives from a superannuation pension or allocated pension that's not treated as taxable income.

⇨ Scenario 2: Wage income of $28000 and no shares.

⇨ Scenario 3: Wage income of $28000 and shares.

⇨ Scenario 4: Wage income of $74000 and no shares.

⇨ Scenario 5: Wage income of $74000 and shares.

The results are shown in table 6.1 (overleaf).

Conclusion

From table 6.1 you can see that people with an income below the threshold level for income tax receive a total percentage return from shares of just over 14.1%. Thereafter the percentage after-tax return from shares decreases as taxable income increases. This is because tax rates increase as income increases.

At taxable income levels where the 30% marginal tax rate applies, dividend income is essentially tax-free because the company tax rate is also 30%. At income levels below this, the shareholder gains additional benefit on franked dividends because the personal tax rate is below the company tax rate. At income levels above this, the dividend won't be completely tax-free but the shareholder will still get a 30% rebate on the dividend income.

Table 6.1: after-tax returns for different scenarios

Scenario	1	2	3	4	5
Portfolio value	100 000	0	100 000	0	100 000
Dividend received	4 000	0	4 000	0	4 000
Franking credit	1 714	0	1 714	0	1 714
Wage income	0	28 000	28 000	74 000	74 000
Total taxable income	5 714	28 000	33 714	74 000	79 714
Tax	0	3 300	4 157	16 050	17 764
After-tax income	**5 714**	**24 700**	**29 557**	**57 950**	**61 950**
Franking credit rebate	1 714	0	1 714	0	1 714
Total after-tax income	**5 714**	**24 700**	**31 271**	**57 950**	**63 664**
Difference in after-tax income*	–	–	6 571	–	5 714
Real difference in after-tax income**	–	–	4 857	–	4 000
Capital gain shares	8 400	–	8 400	–	8 400
Total income shares	14 114	–	13 257	–	12 400
After-tax return on shares	**14.11%**	–	**13.26%**	–	**12.40%**

*   In scenarios 3 and 5, I've calculated the difference in after-tax income for an
      investor with shares and one at the same level of income without shares.

**   The real difference in after-tax income is obtained by deducting the imputation
      credits. I've done this to make the comparison fair, otherwise shares would show
      an even better return. This is because in an income tax return imputation credits
      must be included in a shareholder's taxable income even though they aren't
      received by the shareholder as income (when the shareholder has other taxable
      income apart from shares). Rather the imputation credits are received as a tax
      offset after base tax on the income is calculated.

Building your portfolio with compounding

I'll now show you in table 6.2 how compounding works over
an extended period for a shareholder who doesn't cash in
profits but reinvests all dividend income from shares.

Example 2

Because I don't want to appear as if I'm overstating the case for
shares, I'll assume that the shareholder has considerable wage
income so the percentage return from shares is the lowest in
the range of values from table 6.1; that is, 12.40%.

To help you understand these figures, I've plotted them
on a chart in figure 6.1.

Table 6.2: compounding portfolio and dividend growth

Year	Portfolio value (including reinvested dividends)	Dividend per year	Total dividend
0	100 000	0	0
5	179 404	6 384	25 614
10	321 857	11 454	71 567
15	577 424	20 549	154 008
20	1 035 920	36 865	301 910
25	1 858 480	66 138	567 251
30	3 334 182	118 654	1 043 285

Figure 6.1: compounding portfolio and dividend growth

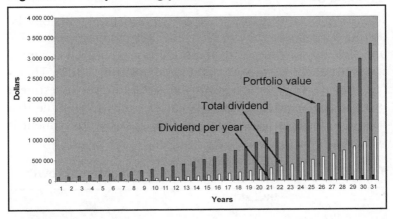

Conclusion

This example demonstrates the power of compounding with a share portfolio over a long time period. At the end of 30 years, the share portfolio has grown in value from $100 000 to over $3.3 million, and the shareholder receives a dividend of nearly $120 000 per year! With a dividend of only 4%, the total dividend income received over this time period is over $1 million!

At this point I hear you say, 'but I haven't got 30 years, that's an awfully long time period'. That's true, but it's not an unrealistic time period if you're relatively young and are prudently thinking of building a nest egg for your retirement. If you find the prospect of long-term investing too daunting, you can still obtain excellent benefits from compounding in the shorter term. For example, from table 6.2 you can see that over 10 years a share portfolio of $100000 has more than tripled in value with the reinvestment of over $70000 in dividend income.

Tip
While compounding works brilliantly in the long term, you can still benefit from compounding in the shorter term.

Example 3

Let's now consider a fixed-interest investment in table 6.3. I'll assume an interest rate on the fixed-interest investment of 7% and that the investor is in the same tax situation I assumed in example 2; that is, with a marginal tax rate of 30%. Therefore the after-tax return from the fixed-interest investment is 4.9%. To make the comparison a fair one, I'll assume that all the after-tax interest from the fixed-interest investment is reinvested.

Table 6.3: compounding fixed-interest investment growth

Year	Investment value (including compounded interest)	Interest per year	Total interest
0	100000	0	0
5	127022	5933	27022
10	161345	7537	61345
15	204943	9573	104943
20	260321	12160	160321
25	330664	15446	230664
30	420015	19619	320015

Conclusion

Comparing table 6.3 with table 6.2, you can see the dramatic difference between the fixed-interest investment and the share investment. After 30 years, the fixed-interest investment has grown in value to about $420 000 compared to the share portfolio value of over $3.3 million!

Tip

Use bank deposits and fixed-interest investments for 'parking' money for the short term only. Share investing is a far better proposition over the longer term.

What if I don't have a substantial share portfolio?

I've explained how to build wealth in the safest and most hassle-free way using the power of compounding with a share portfolio made up of market leading shares. But what if you don't have a substantial share portfolio? What do you do then?

There's no proven get-rich-quick scheme, so the best solution is to start building up your share portfolio as quickly as you can with as much money as you can. The power of compounding really kicks in over the long term so you need to get started as soon as possible. Later on in life, money you invest won't have enough time to build substantially.

One option is to build a substantial share portfolio through regular investing; that is, by periodically buying more shares. I'll show you how this works in the next few examples.

Tip

If you receive a tax refund (or other lump sum of money), use it to buy more shares and build your share portfolio.

Example 4

You have a share portfolio with a value of $10 000. You add to your portfolio by investing an additional $5000 each year.

Using the same assumptions as in example 2, your portfolio will grow as shown in table 6.4.

Table 6.4: portfolio growth adding $5000 each year

Year	Portfolio value (including reinvested dividends)	Dividend	Total dividend
0	10 000	0	0
5	49 958	1 600	4 825
10	121 644	4 151	19 885
15	250 252	8 728	53 307
20	480 979	16 939	119 671
25	894 912	31 669	245 133
30	1 637 524	58 097	476 621

Conclusion

You can see from this table that after 10 years your portfolio will be valued at over $120 000, after 20 years over $480 000 and after 30 years over $1.6 million.

Increasing the amount invested each year

If you can increase the amount you add to your portfolio each year, the growth in your wealth will be more dramatic. This is a realistic scenario if you're earning a wage or salary, because it's reasonable to expect your income to increase as time goes on. So the proportion of your income you can set aside for investing should also increase as time goes on.

Example 5

You start with a portfolio value of $10 000 and buy an additional $5000 worth of shares in the first year. Thereafter, you plan to increase the amount you add to your portfolio by 5% each year. So, in the following year you'll buy an additional $5250 worth of shares, and then $5512.50 worth the next year and so on. If you follow this plan your wealth will grow as shown in table 6.5.

Table 6.5: portfolio growth adding $5000 + 5% per year

Year	Portfolio value (including reinvested dividends)	Invested amount	Dividend	Total dividend
0	10 000	5 000	0	0
5	52 924	6 381	1 667	4 934
10	139 596	8 144	4 692	21 518
15	307 425	10 395	10 588	61 140
20	624 261	13 266	21 766	144 817
25	1 212 770	16 932	42 585	311 011
30	2 294 221	21 610	80 912	629 686

Conclusion

In this case, after 10 years your portfolio will have grown to nearly $140 000, after 20 years to over $624 000 and after 30 years will be nudging $2.3 million.

Tip

The time to start building your wealth is right now! The more you can increase your invested capital each year, the more your wealth will build in future years.

Financial targets

You should now be in a position to create financial targets for your share investing. It's far better to set concrete financial targets and work towards the achievement of those targets than to simply have a fuzzy idea such as, 'I'll make as much money as I can from shares'. It's a fact that performance improves when people work towards achievement of concrete, predetermined targets rather than just trying to do their best.

Tip

Set financial targets for your share investing and work towards the achievement of those targets. Put your plan in writing and refer to it from time to time.

Your plan

At a minimum, your investing plan should include the following details:

⇨ how much of your available investment capital will be initially allocated to shares

⇨ how much capital (over and above dividend payments) you plan to invest in shares each year

⇨ the time period of your investment

⇨ the end point; that is, the value you'd like your share portfolio to have at the end of the time period.

Tip

The most logical way of setting your financial targets is to work backwards from the end point.

Financial calculator spreadsheet

The tables and numerical examples I've used in this chapter should provide a guide for your planning. A good option is to set up a spreadsheet because this enables you to customise your plan to suit your own financial situation. Once you've set up the spreadsheet you can vary the data and see how this affects the end result.

I'll now show you how you can set up your own financial calculator spreadsheet (see figure 6.2). The spreadsheet program I've used is Microsoft Excel. (The first five rows are read from left to right, so row 1 is 'Initial portfolio value', row 2 is 'Amount added year 1' and so on.)

Figure 6.2: financial calculator spreadsheet

	A	B	C	D	E
1	Initial	portfolio	value	$	
2	Amount	added	year 1	$	
3	Capital	growth	per year	%	
4	Dividend	yield	per year	%	
5	Increase	amt added	per year	%	
6	Year	Portfolio value	Amt added	Dividend	Total dividend
7	0	= E1	= E2	0	0
8	1	Formula B8	Formula C8	Formula D8	Formula E8
9	2	Copy down	Copy down	Copy down	Copy down
10	"	"	"	"	"

Notes:

- The formula in cell B8 is: = B7*(1+($E$3+$E$4)/100)+C7
- The formula in cell C8 is: = C7*(1+$E$5/100)
- The formula in cell D8 is: = B7*$E$4/100
- The formula in cell E8 is: = D8+E7
- In cells E1 to E5 you insert the data relevant to your own financial situation.
- After you've inserted the formulas I've given in row 8, copy down and Excel automatically copies the formulas and changes the row numbers for as many lines as you want for the number of years required.
- You need to adjust the number of decimal places. You can do this easily in Excel using the 'Reduce decimal' button. I've set my spreadsheet up so that whole numbers only are displayed (that is, dollars and no cents).
- You may wish to format large numbers with commas to make them easier to read.
- Once you've set up the spreadsheet, you can vary the data and see the effect on the final value of your portfolio and dividend income, and in this way you can set your financial targets.
- You can use the spreadsheet for any compounding financial investment by inserting the initial investment amount in cell E1 and using the interest rate in place of dividend yield.

Example 6

Let's use the spreadsheet with the data given in example 5 over a 10-year period.

Solution

Initial	portfolio	value	$	10 000
Amount	added	year 1	$	5 000
Capital	growth	per year	%	8.4
Dividend	yield	per year	%	4
Increase	amt added	per year	%	5
Year	Portfolio value	Amt added	Dividend	Total dividend
0	10 000	5 000	0	0
1	16 240	5 250	400	400
2	23 504	5 513	650	1 050
3	31 931	5 788	940	1 990
4	41 678	6 078	1 277	3 267
5	52 924	6 381	1 667	4 934
6	65 868	6 700	2 117	7 051
7	80 736	7 036	2 635	9 686
8	97 783	7 387	3 229	12 915
9	117 295	7 757	3 911	16 827
10	139 596	8 144	4 692	21 518

Modifying the financial spreadsheet

The financial spreadsheet understates portfolio and dividend growth; that is, it errs on the conservative side. Can you see why?

The reason is that I've set the spreadsheet up on an annual basis, so all returns are annual returns. In fact, dividends are usually paid twice a year, and if you reinvest dividends the final dividend at the end of the year will be greater than that shown by the spreadsheet. This is because of the effect of compounding—the interim dividend reinvested increases the second dividend.

If you want to take this complication into account, you can easily modify the spreadsheet by using six-monthly periods rather than years. When you insert the data, you need to halve the returns each six months. I'll show you how this works in the next example.

Example 7

Let's use the spreadsheet to recalculate the results over a 10-year period but this time using six-monthly dividends.

Solution

I won't show the full set of calculations, just those applicable to period 10 (that is, after five years) and period 20 (that is, after 10 years).

Initial	portfolio	value	$	10 000
Amount	added	year 1	$	2 500
Capital	growth	per year	%	4.2
Dividend	yield	per year	%	2
Increase	amt added	per year	%	2.5
Period	Portfolio value	Amt added	Dividend	Total dividend
0	10 000	2 500	0	0
10	55 063	3 200	978	5 501
20	147 610	4 097	2 705	23 790

You can see that after five years (10 periods), the portfolio will have a value of $55 063, rather than $52 924 calculated previously. After 10 years (20 periods), the value is $147 610, rather than $139 596 as calculated previously. So you can see that by receiving dividends every six months rather than each year you considerably increase your portfolio growth and dividends. However (and in the interests of simplicity) you may still want to do the calculation on an annual basis and err on the conservative side.

Chapter summary

⇨ Historically, Australian shares have provided an excellent level of return for investors. When dividends, franking credits and capital gains are included, the percentage return has averaged about 14.1% over the last 30 years.

⇨ An actual 14.1% return after tax is achievable for investors with income below the company tax level. As income increases, increasing tax rates reduce the after-tax return.

⇨ If total taxable income is such that the investor is paying tax at the marginal rate of 30%, the after-tax return from shares reduces to 12.4%. Currently, the threshold income level for this rate of tax is $80 000 per annum.

⇨ By reinvesting dividends, a share portfolio returning 12.4% would increase in value from $100 000 to over $320 000 after 10 years, to over $1 million in 20 years and to over $3 million in 30 years.

⇨ A fixed-interest investment produces a far lower return than shares over the longer term. This is because there's no capital growth and there are no franking credits associated with the interest payments.

⇨ Use bank deposits and fixed-interest investments only for 'parking' money over the relatively short term.

⇨ The sooner you can start building a share portfolio the better. Consider using any available funds, such as a taxation refund, to add to your share portfolio.

⇨ If you don't have a substantial portfolio of shares, try to set aside an amount each year to build up your portfolio. For example, by buying $5000 worth of shares each year and reinvesting dividends, you can build a portfolio of $10 000 to over $120 000 in 10 years and to over $480 000 in 20 years.

⇨ It's very important to set financial targets and to have a plan that will enable you to achieve those targets. I've included a spreadsheet format that you can set up on your computer that allows you to vary invested amounts and levels of return to better set future targets and set out a plan for achievement of those targets.

chapter 7

Diversifying your share investment

In this chapter I look at the second principle of my long-term investing strategy; that is, diversifying your investment in shares. I'll discuss how you can do so effectively.

As outlined in chapter 5, you can diversify your investment capital into various asset classes such as shares, bonds, fixed-interest accounts and property. As a reader of this book, I assume you're primarily interested in investing in Australian shares so I'm not going to discuss and compare the other asset classes in detail, other than to say that you should always keep some of your investment capital in readily accessible cash. This is because you never know when the market might turn down, and if it does cash is king. When the market recovers after a downturn (and the Australian sharemarket always has done so), there can be some excellent buying opportunities available. But you can't take advantage of them if you don't have some cash available.

Tip

Keep around 20% of your investment capital in cash —particularly in times of high economic uncertainty and market volatility.

Reducing risk

The main reason why you should consider diversifying your share investment is to reduce risk. Let's consider one particular approach to risk management.

The 'Swiss cheese' approach to risk management

The 'Swiss cheese' approach can be used in almost any situation to reduce the risk of failure. For example, it's been used with great success in the airline industry to reduce the risk that some vital component of an aircraft will malfunction.

This approach is called the Swiss cheese approach because you can imagine a risk management strategy as a slice of cheese. Because no risk management strategy is perfect, there are a number of holes in the slice and these represent the possibility of failure. If the strategy is 90% effective, there's a 10% risk of failure and this would be a slice of Swiss cheese where the area of the holes is 10% of the area of the slice.

But what happens if we take two slices at random from different packets of Swiss cheese and put one behind the other? I've represented this in figure 7.1.

Suppose the second slice of cheese has the same area of holes as the first slice (10%). If a problem passes through a hole in the first slice, the second slice will stop it going any further unless two holes happen to line up. What's the chance of this happening? You might think that with two slices there'd be half the risk—that is, 5%—but in fact the risk reduces to only 1%. This is because the probabilities are multiplied, as follows:

$0.1 \times 0.1 = 0.01$ or 1%

Figure 7.1: Swiss cheese approach to managing risk

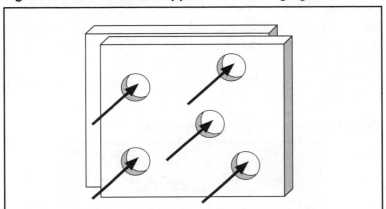

If there were three slices, the risk would reduce to only 0.1% or 1 in a 1000.

You'd be quite justified in thinking that a 1 in 1000 risk is still too high for an aircraft. Today airlines aim for a failure risk below 1 in a million. For the purpose of the calculation above I assumed a risk of failure in a single component or system of 10%, but of course that would be totally unacceptable in an aircraft. Quality systems should ensure a risk of below 1 in 1000, so with a single back-up system the risk reduces to 1 in a million, and with another back-up system 1 in a billion.

Using the Swiss cheese approach with shares

The Swiss cheese approach is a risk management technique that can be applied to a share portfolio. You can think of each slice of cheese as being a different company (or stock) in your portfolio and the holes in each slice as representing the risk of failure (underperformance). The more slices (stocks) you hold, the lower the overall risk of underperformance. For example, suppose your share selection strategy is only 50% successful. It's a slice of Swiss cheese where the area of the holes is 50% of the slice area. I think you'll agree that you haven't chosen a great strategy because there's as much risk of failure as there is of success with any one stock. In this situation, with only one stock the risk of failure is 50%. This risk is known as tracking risk or tracking error. But what happens if you increase the number of different stocks in your portfolio without changing your stock selection strategy?

Table 7.1 and figure 7.2 show the outcome of adding more stocks to this strategy.

Table 7.1: effect of adding more stocks

Number of stocks	Probability	Percentage tracking error
1	0.5	50
2	0.25	25
3	0.125	12.5
4	0.0625	6.25
5	0.03125	3.125
6	0.015625	1.56
7	0.0078125	0.78
8	0.00390625	0.39
9	0.001953125	0.20
10	0.000976563	0.10

This graph clearly shows the benefits of diversification. Even using a selection strategy that's only 50% effective, with five different stocks in your portfolio the likelihood of all of them underperforming is only about 3%, and with 10 different stocks the likelihood is only about 0.1%!

Tip

A benefit of diversification is that one good overperforming share can more than compensate for a number of under-performing ones.

Figure 7.2: effect of adding more stocks

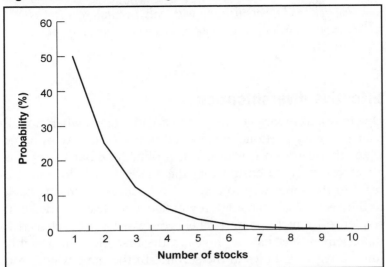

How many stocks should you hold?

Another conclusion evident from figure 7.2 is that the law of diminishing returns applies and the risk reduction benefit quickly tapers off as the number of stocks increases. By increasing the number of stocks from one to five you get a 47% risk reduction, but by holding five more you get an additional benefit of less than 3%. So the good news is that you don't need to hold a large number of different stocks to get good risk management.

I've read share investing books where the author has recommended you hold at least 20 different stocks in your portfolio. In principle, the more the better in terms of diversification, but on the other hand the more different stocks you own the more effort and time you'll need to maintain records and keep up to date with developments. That's contrary to our aim, which is to simplify sharemarket investing — so why complicate the issue if the additional complication doesn't produce any significant benefit?

Tip

You get good diversification with only five different stocks in your portfolio and you get excellent diversification with 10.

Effective diversification

Diversification works to reduce risk with shares when not all shares in your portfolio are affected in the same way by some event that causes a downturn in profitability. But to get this effect you need to ensure that the shares you hold don't all react in the same way to external influences. Thinking back to the Swiss cheese analogy, if you take two slices of cheese in sequence from the same packet, you won't get effective risk management because the holes in the first slice will roughly line up with the holes in the second. In the same way, if you hold different stocks in the same sector (type of industry), they'll most likely react in similar fashion to economic events and you won't get effective diversification. However, you should still get some benefit if an event affects one company and not others, such as the loss of a major customer or contract or a disastrous fire in a warehouse. To get really effective diversification you need to hold shares that are in different market sectors so they won't all be affected in the same way when a significant change occurs.

Tip

To diversify effectively you need to hold shares of companies that are in different market sectors.

Example 1

As an example, consider the big four banks, which in order of market value (at the time of writing) are Commonwealth, Westpac, NAB and ANZ. Let's look at the relative performance of the top two—Commonwealth (CBA) and Westpac (WBC) —compared to the All Ords index (XAO) over a one-year period to the end of November 2009. I've drawn a percentage chart in figure 7.3 so it's easy to compare performance.

You can see how the price rises and falls tend to be synchronised. The same type of chart drawn for NAB and ANZ shows a very similar result.

Figure 7.3: CBA, WBC and XAO relative performance

Source: www.CommSec.com.au / Wall St on Demand

During this one-year period, the big four banks and the All Ords index performed as follows:

⇨ XAO up 13%

⇨ CBA up 32%

⇨ WBC up 23%

⇨ NAB up 18%

⇨ ANZ up 22%.

Conclusion

The following conclusions can be drawn:

⇨ Each of the big four banks outperformed the general sharemarket.

⇨ Commonwealth Bank was the standout performer.

⇨ Each of the other three performed similarly and rose by 20% ± 3%.

⇨ A portfolio consisting of just the big four banks wouldn't be an effectively diversified one.

Example 2

Let's now look at the relative performance of one of the largest energy stocks, Santos (STO), compared to the Common-wealth Bank and the All Ords index. I've shown the chart in figure 7.4.

Figure 7.4: STO, CBA and XAO relative performance

Source: www.CommSec.com.au / Wall St on Demand

You now see a totally different picture because the rises and falls are not synchronised; the performance of Santos was very different from that of CBA and XAO.

Conclusion

Including an energy stock such as Santos in a portfolio with Commonwealth Bank would provide better diversification than including another major bank stock in the portfolio.

Sector diversification

Diversification by holding shares in different banking stocks isn't very effective because they're all in the same sector. There will be some differences in performance due to factors such as differences in management (from the board of directors down to regional managers), policies and procedures, location of offices and branches, customers, size and available capital and resources. Despite these differences, there are many factors that tend to affect all banking stocks in a very similar way, such as global and Australian economic events, changes to government policy, the level of inflation and household debt.

To achieve really effective diversification, you need to think in terms of sector diversification and select stocks for your portfolio that are in different industries. The ASX has adopted the Global Industry Classification Standard (GICS), and at the time of writing it consisted of 14 different sectors into which all Australian shares are grouped. Like shares, each sector is identified using a three-letter code; for example, the financial sector is identified using the code XFJ.

Tip

A complete listing of Australian industry sectors can be found on the ASX website and in my books Teach Yourself About Shares *and* Online Investing on the Australian Sharemarket.

The downside of diversification

I don't want to leave you with the impression that diversification is all good news because there's also a downside. Diversification reduces the risk (or probability) of under-performance of a share portfolio, but at the same time diversification reduces the likelihood of overperformance. In other words, the more diversified your portfolio, the less likely it is that you'll be able to outperform the market.

The only way you can outperform the market is through portfolio concentration. If you're very clever (or lucky) and choose only a few stocks for your portfolio and these shares do better than the market, your portfolio as a whole will outperform the market. As discussed above, if your portfolio consisted of only one or two of the major banks, in the one-year period to around the end of November 2009 your portfolio would have outperformed the market by a considerable margin. In fact, if you held only Commonwealth Bank shares your portfolio would have outperformed the market by 19%, because CBA went up 32% compared to the All Ords which went up 13%.

On the other hand, if you're not so clever (or lucky), a concentrated portfolio has greater potential for under-performance. According to the efficient market hypothesis it's very difficult (if not impossible) to consistently beat the market over the long term.

So really, I don't think it's a disadvantage that your portfolio tracks the market fairly closely. However, there may be some readers still intent on beating the market. For those readers, concentration rather than diversification is the name of the game.

Chapter summary

⇨ You can diversify by investing in different asset classes, such as property, fixed-interest investments and shares.

⇨ It's a good idea to keep a proportion of your investment capital in readily accessible cash, particularly in times of high economic uncertainty and market volatility.

⇨ You can think of risk management with shares using the 'Swiss cheese' analogy, where the holes in each slice represent failure points. The greater the number of different slices the lower the overall failure risk.

⇨ You can diversify your share investment by holding a number of different stocks.

⇨ Diversification is most effective when you invest in companies from different industry sectors.

⇨ The Australian sharemarket has 14 different industry sectors that are aligned to the Global Industry Classification Standard.

⇨ Diversification reduces the risk of underperformance of your portfolio but it also reduces the likelihood of overperformance.

⇨ The law of diminishing returns applies to diversification; holding a large number of different stocks won't produce much additional benefit. Indeed, it may be a counterproductive exercise to have a large number of different stocks as this increases the time and effort required to properly manage your portfolio.

⇨ You can obtain effective diversification with five stocks taken from different industry sectors. Ten stocks spread over different sectors will provide excellent diversification.

chapter 8

Investing in shares with good fundamentals

In this chapter I discuss in greater detail shares to consider for your portfolio. As I outlined in chapter 5, the safest option for a long-term portfolio is good-quality Australian shares, so let's now look more closely at these.

Good-quality shares

I'll now summarise 10 criteria that will help you recognise good-quality shares with strong fundamentals, and then I'll consider each one in a little more detail. I'll show you how to research these criteria in later chapters.

Criteria

1   The shares are fully paid ordinary shares (or units) listed on the ASX.

2   The company has been operating for a considerable period and is not a 'Johnny-come-lately'. Its products

(whether goods or services or both) are well regarded in the marketplace; that is, they have good market acceptance.

3 Preferably, the company operates primarily in Australia.

4 The shares are liquid.

5 The shares trade at a relatively high price.

6 The company has a high market capitalisation.

7 The company has a history of continued good profitability over a reasonably long period.

8 The company pays a reasonable dividend to shareholders —preferably fully franked—and has done so for some years.

9 The company has a strong balance sheet; that is, relatively low debt compared to assets.

10 The company has stable and reputable directors and management executives.

I'll now discuss each of these criteria in detail.

1 *The shares are fully paid ordinary shares (or units) listed on the ASX.*

Firstly, I'll clear up the distinction between shares and units. Businesses can be set up or legally constituted in several ways, of which the most common are:

⇨ sole proprietor

⇨ partnership

⇨ private company

⇨ public company

⇨ trust

⇨ cooperative.

For investing purposes we're concerned with listed public companies and listed trusts only. There's a legal distinction between them that we needn't go into, except to say that listed public companies issue shares whereas listed trusts issue units. For investing purposes there's really no difference as they are quoted on the ASX in the same way and traded in the same way. In common language (and in this book) the word 'shares' means shares or units.

Fully paid ordinary shares are the most common type of shares. The best way of distinguishing them from any other types is that the others are identified by additional descriptors and the share code will contain more than three letters. Other listed instruments include:

⇨ preference shares

⇨ contributing shares

⇨ hybrids

⇨ options

⇨ rights.

The ASX is the main stock exchange in Australia. There is another stock exchange that operates in Australia, namely the National Stock Exchange (NSX). It concentrates on listing small to medium-sized companies and financial products. Information and share prices are not as readily available for these as for enterprises listed on the ASX, and not all brokers operate on the NSX. For these reasons I suggest you stick to shares listed on the ASX.

Tip

I suggest you stick to fully paid ordinary shares (or units) only. Other listed instruments are suitable only for experienced traders.

2   *The company has been operating for a considerable
    period and is not a 'Johnny-come-lately'. Its products
    (whether goods or services or both) are well regarded
    in the marketplace; that is, they have good market
    acceptance.*

When a new-venture company first floats (issues shares) it
can be an opportunity to buy shares at a cheap price that may
later increase considerably. However, it's also true that buying
shares in a new-venture company is risky because:

⇨ there's no proven track record over an extended period

⇨ the new venture may not be successful, either because
the product doesn't achieve market acceptance or
because the management may not be to best practice
level.

For these reasons, it's safer to stick to companies with well-
known products.

If the company's products are marketed to consumers,
you'll most likely be familiar with the company. Often they'll
advertise their products via newspapers and magazines,
television and radio, or on billboards. They'll usually have
outlets in most Australian states and territories.

For example, most Australians would be aware of com-
panies such as AMP, ANZ Bank, ASX, BHP Billiton, Billabong,
Caltex, Coca-Cola Amatil, Commonwealth Bank, David Jones,
Fairfax Media, Foster's, Harvey Norman, Myer Holdings,
National Australia Bank, Newscorp, Qantas, Santos, Soul
Pattinson, Tabcorp, Telstra, Wesfarmers, Westfield Group,
Westpac Bank and Woolworths—to name just a few.

Companies supplying products to industry may not be as
familiar to you because they won't advertise as widely or have
retail outlets. Most of the mining and resource companies
fall into this category. Nevertheless, you'll probably know of
companies such as Alcoa, Aluminia, Bluescope Steel, Boral,
Brambles, Coal & Allied, Computershare, CSL, ERA, Downer

EDI, Fortescue Metals, Leighton Holdings, Lihir Gold, Metcash, Nufarm, Onesteel, Oz Minerals, Primary Health Care, Rio Tinto, Toll Holdings and Woodside Petroleum.

There may be some good-quality Australian companies you aren't familiar with, but with a little research you can easily find out how long the company has been operating.

Tip

Unless you're a seasoned trader, it's best to avoid little-known, speculative stocks and stick to well-known and respected companies selling products that have a proven track record of success.

3   Preferably, the company operates primarily in Australia.

I prefer to invest in companies that operate primarily in Australia because Australia has a history of stable and reputable government and peaceful coexistence with one another and our neighbours—unlike some countries that have a chequered history of unstable governments and civil unrest. Also the Australian economy has a history of growth and expansion that looks set to continue.

There are some exceptions with ASX-listed companies that operate outside Australia which shouldn't be automatically excluded from a portfolio. For example, Lihir Gold operates primarily in Papua New Guinea but its shares have been excellent performers on the Australian market for many years. Other Australian companies with overseas ventures have fared less well, such as the highly respected National Australia Bank which lost a great deal of money when it ventured into Great Britain. Similarly Brambles has not had continuing success with its US operations and Foster's ended up with burnt fingers when it paid a considerable sum to take over the Beringer winery in the US.

Our close neighbour New Zealand also has a history of stability in its government and economy, and many Australian companies have branches in New Zealand (for example, ANZ Bank). That's fine by me, provided their main operations are in Australia.

Tip

Shares in companies operating primarily in Australia are usually less risky.

4 The shares are liquid.

The number of shares that change hands each day is known as volume. Liquid shares have a high volume whereas illiquid shares trade infrequently and have a low volume.

The main benefit of trading liquid shares is obvious: shares, like any commodity, can trade only if there's a willing buyer and a willing seller at an agreed price. Liquid shares are easy to trade at any time because there are always many buyers and sellers, so you can readily trade whenever you want. This eliminates the risk that you might be stuck with shares you want to sell, or not be able to buy shares you want, because you can't trade at a reasonable price.

Another advantage of trading liquid shares is that the spread is usually small, and often no more than a cent or so. Spread is the difference between the highest bid price of buyers and the lowest offer price of sellers. For example, if the highest bid price of a share is $9.54 and the lowest offer price is $9.55, the spread is 1¢. The benefit of a low spread is that you can trade readily without having to pay a substantial premium when you buy or take a substantial drop in price when you sell.

Tip

Major shares traded on the ASX are usually very liquid and many thousands (or even millions) of shares change hands each day. This means you can buy or sell them at a reasonable price whenever you want.

5   The shares trade at a relatively high price.

It's almost always the case that if a company is a well-respected major player in Australia its shares will trade at a relatively high price. Cheap shares are known colloquially as 'penny dreadfuls', as they trade in cents or even fractions of a cent rather than in dollars. They're also the more speculative types of shares, and if you trade them you're venturing into the high-risk area of speculation (or even gambling) compared to investing.

There's a perception among traders that fast money can be made trading speculative shares because they tend to be volatile and there can be large rises or falls in price in a short period of time. Also simple mathematics indicates that cheaper shares have a higher potential profit margin with small price moves. For example, if a share trading for 10¢ goes up 5¢ in price, the profit margin is 50%. However, if a share trading for $1.00 goes up 5¢, the same price rise results in only a 5% profit margin.

While this is true, it's also evident that losses can occur more quickly if the price moves in the wrong direction. For example, if a share trading for 10¢ goes down in price by 9¢, the loss is 90%. Even worse, the price can fall to a fraction of a cent and then the loss is almost 100%. That's by no means a rare event with really speculative shares that trade on a wing and a prayer (and blue sky potential) rather than on a well-established business profile.

Tip

Low-priced shares are usually of the more speculative type, and while there's the potential for high and quick profitability, they're more risky and best avoided in a long-term investment portfolio.

6   The company has a high market capitalisation.

Market capitalisation (commonly abbreviated to market cap) is a way of determining the size of a listed company from a share investor's viewpoint. It's the total amount of money that's invested in the shares issued by the company, and it's calculated by multiplying the number of issued shares by the share price (market price). The mathematical formula is:

Market cap = Number of issued shares × Share price

Usually the number of issued shares used for the market cap calculation takes into account ordinary shares only, but it may also include some dilution allowance for options and rights. These aren't shares as such but give the holder the right to convert the option or right into a fully paid ordinary share at some time in the future.

Market capitalisation is calculated using the market price, and because it fluctuates with each trade the market cap is continually changing and is valid only at a given point in time.

As you can see, market cap is a financial statistic that's based only on the number of shares and the share price. It doesn't take into account many other factors that are normally associated with the relative size of a business, such as:

⇨ number of employees

⇨ physical size in terms of the number of branches or operating divisions

⇨ dollar value of product sales (turnover)

⇨ amount of profit made

⇨ value of the company assets.

Even though the market cap calculation doesn't directly take into account the above factors, generally speaking all these factors will be large for companies with high market caps. That's to say, a company with a high market cap will usually have a large number of employees, be a large organisation, will have a high product turnover, will make large profits and have high-value assets. Companies that have a high market cap are major players and are well-known and respected companies.

Tip

For share investing purposes, when companies are ranked as major players, market leaders or top companies the ranking is usually according to market cap. Market leaders have a high market cap that's always many billions of dollars. When you own shares in these companies you're getting with the strength.

7 The company has a history of continued good profitability over a reasonably long period.

Companies that have a history of continued good profitability are generally sound ones to invest in. Past earnings help to build a solid foundation for the future, and I'll explain why.

When a company makes a profit, what does it do with the money? To answer this question, consider your own situation. Suppose you receive a windfall of some sort—perhaps a substantial tax refund, a lottery win or money from an estate. What are you going to do with the money? There are really only three options:

⇨ spend the money

⇨ keep the money (retain it)

⇨ spend some and retain some.

A company has exactly the same choices when it comes to profits:

⇨ The company can spend the money by distributing it to shareholders in the form of a dividend. The directors and executives may also be given a profit-based incentive payment.

⇨ The company can keep the profit and distribute none to shareholders or executives.

⇨ The company can pay out some of the profit and keep the rest.

Most profitable companies in Australia generally choose the third option and distribute some profit to shareholders (and executives) and retain the rest in the business. The percentage distributed to shareholders is known as the payout ratio and it's usually between 50% and 70%. This means that the company retains between 30% and 50% of its earnings.

Using retained profits

When profits are retained in a business, what do the directors do with the money? The retained profits are generally rein-vested back in the business and used for some useful purpose such as:

⇨ upgrading assets

⇨ investing in new technology to improve productivity

⇨ reducing debt

⇨ expanding the business.

Using profits in these ways helps to maintain profitability in the future and so lays the foundation for sustained earn-ings growth. This means that an investor today can actually profit from past earnings if these profits have been reinvested wisely.

Tip

While you can't profit from past dividends or capital gains directly, reinvested profits from past earnings help to ensure future profitability. A company with a good track record of profitability is generally a good one to invest in.

8 *The company pays a reasonable dividend to shareholders—preferably fully franked—and has done so for some years.*

Firstly, I'll explain 'reasonable dividend'; by this I mean that the shares have a relatively high yield. (At this stage you might like to refresh your understanding of dividends and yields by referring back to chapter 2.)

I prefer to invest in companies that pay a reasonable dividend, but I need to point out that it's a personal preference and there's been much debate over the years about whether or not dividends are desirable for investors. Some investment advisers advocate buying shares that don't pay a dividend on the grounds that if the company doesn't pay a dividend it's retaining all profits in the business. The claimed benefit is that over a period of time the retained dividends will increase the value of the business and result in an increased share price, rewarding investors because they're obtaining higher capital gains than would otherwise be the case.

It's an argument that sounds good in theory but in my experience it's not one that bears out in practice. For example, during the financial crisis of 2008–09 shares throughout the world were sold off and prices plunged. In the Australian market, the All Ords dived about 50% (please refer to figure 4.1 on p. 52). However, in the aftermath of the crisis as share prices recovered again the banking sector led the recovery with outstanding gains. For example, Commonwealth Bank was a stellar performer, and after bottoming the price doubled in six months or so. Yet Commonwealth Bank consistently paid good dividends before, during and after the crisis. As another example, consider the mining and exploration sector where companies seldom pay dividends. I've seen no evidence that investors have made better capital gains with mining and exploration shares than they have with shares in the industrial sector where many companies pay good dividends.

I believe that part of the reason why you can still make good capital gains with companies that pay dividends is that most investors like to receive dividends and therefore there's a higher demand for shares in companies that pay reasonable dividends than in companies that don't. And as we know, increased demand drives share prices higher and results in capital gains for investors.

Another reason I value dividends is that a company needs to make a good profit to be able to pay a reasonable dividend, so a company paying a good dividend is almost always a profitable one. A company may pay a reasonable dividend even though it's making a loss, but this is rare and cannot be sustained as no loss-making company can pay good dividends over any length of time. So a company that consistently pays a good dividend must be making enough profit to pay the dividend and still maintain the profitability of the business. In other words, it's a sound, well-run company and the type in which I want to own shares.

As I've outlined before, I prefer a franked income to an unfranked one because dividend franking is an excellent tax benefit that provides an inbuilt tax concession. However, a high unfranked dividend could be better than a lower franked one; to compare them you need to gross up the franked dividend to obtain an equivalent unfranked one. I explained how to do this in chapter 2.

Tip

A company that consistently pays a good dividend is almost always making consistently good profits and is usually a good company for long-term investing.

9 The company has a strong balance sheet; that is, relatively low debt compared to assets.

As I pointed out in chapter 5, a company with a large amount of debt is potentially more risky than one with low debt levels. If business is booming high debt is not a problem, but should a downturn occur high debt can bankrupt a business.

The reason for this becomes clear if you consider your own financial situation. If you have a large mortgage and/or other debts, you're relying on continuing income to pay your debt obligations (interest and loan repayments). If that income should decline for any reason and you're unable to keep up the loan repayments, you could be in dire straits should the bank (or other lending institution) threaten foreclosure. In fact, that's exactly what caused the global financial crisis of 2008–09, when banks and lending institutions (chiefly in the US) lent too much money in the form of sub-prime mortgages; that is, giving mortgages to people who didn't have good creditworthiness and sufficient equity. It took only a relatively small downturn in the economy for some of these people to lose income and default on their loans. The lending institutions foreclosed and the properties were put on the market. But as more and more properties were put up for sale, property prices fell because supply exceeded demand. Then the banks and financial institutions couldn't recover their money and their losses mounted, until inevitably bankruptcy followed. Once the downward spiral started, it gathered pace until the whole world eventually became embroiled in a financial calamity.

Any business with a high level of debt is in a precarious financial situation. As long as business is booming it can continue to pay its debt obligations and still make a profit, but should there be any downturn in sales or profits it could be in trouble. Companies with large amounts of debt are essentially risky, so why take the risk by investing in these companies if you don't need to?

Tip

Companies that have large amounts of debt in comparison to their assets are said to be highly geared, and are inherently more risky because a downturn in business can trigger financial difficulties.

There are several ways you can evaluate the level of debt in a business. Some of the common ones are:

⇨ debt to equity ratio

⇨ interest cover

⇨ current ratio.

Debt to equity ratio

The debt to equity ratio is obtained by dividing the long-term debt by shareholder equity, and is usually expressed as a percentage. The lower the debt to equity ratio, the lower the gearing and the lower the risk.

In this calculation long-term debt (also known as interest-bearing debt) is used. It's the amount of loan capital (capital obtained from long-term loans). Shareholder equity is also known as proprietorship (or net assets) and is the total assets less liabilities. That's to say, shareholder equity is the value of what's left over when the liabilities are subtracted from the assets (and so the term net assets).

Interest cover

Interest cover is a measure of how much profit the company makes (before interest on loans and tax) compared to the amount of interest paid on long-term loans. Clearly if a company makes only enough profit to pay interest on loans, it's just keeping its head above water and there's nothing left over—not a good option from an investor's viewpoint. The greater the interest cover the safer the business and the greater the amount of after-tax profit that can be used to expand the business and reward shareholders with a dividend.

Current ratio

The current ratio is the ratio of current assets (or short-term assets) compared to current or short-term liabilities. It's not a measure of gearing in the same way as the debt to equity ratio or interest cover because it's based on short-term rather than long-term debt. So it's a measure of the ability of the business to meet immediate debt obligations.

To understand the distinction, think about your own situation. Owning valuable long-term assets such as your own home won't help you pay the electricity or phone bill due this month. Long-term assets don't help pay short-term debt obligations because they can't readily be converted into cash. So a company needs to have a current ratio greater than 1.0 so it can meet its immediate debt obligations with readily available cash.

Tip

The safest companies from an investor's viewpoint are those with low gearing (as measured by the debt to equity ratio), high interest cover and a current ratio greater than 1.0.

After this discussion you might be wondering if it's best to invest in companies with little or no long-term debt obligations; that is, companies that don't use business loans as a source of capital. Interestingly, it's generally to shareholders' advantage if a company does have a significant amount of loan capital as long as it's not an excessive proportion of total capital. The reasons for this are explained in detail in a self-test exercise in *Teach Yourself About Shares*, chapter 8.

10 The company has stable and reputable directors and management executives.

Finally, we come to the most important investing criteria of all: to have a competent team of management executives. I can't overemphasise the importance of a good board of directors and top management. In the past I've invested in companies that were basically sound because I liked their products, for which I foresaw a growing market. Yet many times these companies didn't fulfil my expectations and I ended up selling my shares for a loss. The inevitable conclusion that follows is that these companies were poorly managed.

There's a high failure rate with new businesses in Australia, and those that survive and prosper are those that are well managed and profitable. Apart from all other considerations, the bottom line is that a company must be profitable and produce a better return than is achievable from bonds or fixed-interest investments, otherwise there's no point to its existence.

Shareholders are the owners of the company and they elect the board of directors, whose primary function is to guide the company to profitability and to make ethical decisions that are in the best interests of the shareholders. The board of directors usually comprises members who aren't full-time employees and who meet only when there's a board meeting or company general meeting. There may be one or more managing directors who are full-time employees in the company as well as being appointed to the board, but usually the majority of the management executives aren't board members but are appointed by the board and are accountable to the board for their performance.

Case study

As an example, consider the disastrous case of ABC Learning Centres. During its time in the sun many financial analysts and advisers were urging investors to buy shares in this company. I considered doing so myself (but fortunately didn't) because one of my grandchildren was attending an ABC centre and I was impressed by the cleanliness, adherence to OHS and environmental standards and overall efficiency that was evident at this centre. The company was servicing a growing market resulting from a trend for both parents to work to provide the income required to service increasing home mortgage repayments resulting from increasing property values. The company was expanding, with more centres being opened each year throughout Australia.

Great product, apparently sound company, expanding demand; all ingredients for success. The sharemarket agreed, and the share price trended upward for a considerable time. Then suddenly and unexpectedly, the company went into liquidation with huge debts it couldn't repay. The shares plummeted and many investors lost all. The inevitable con-clusion is that the business wasn't well-managed financially at the top executive level. Clearly, the directors were over-ambitious and stretched the company finances past the point of no return.

Tip

A sound product and a growing demand for the product don't necessarily guarantee the success of a business. Continuing profitability can be achieved only if the company is well managed at top executive level by directors who have the long-term interests of shareholders at heart.

Evaluating directorship

While sound directorship is a most important ingredient in the long-term success of any business, it's also a difficult factor to evaluate because, unlike financial statistics, there's no numerical rating for directors and generally little guidance available for investors. You can't look up statistics indicating that the board of a company has a certain management score (say 70%). So the evaluation must be subjective rather than objective, and it's one you have to make for yourself.

It's easy enough to find out who the directors are as this information is readily available; for example, on company websites and in annual reports. Once you know who the directors are, you can search the internet (for example, a Google search of each director) to establish their credentials and track record.

Some factors you can consider when rating directors are:

⇨ What are their qualifications?

⇨ How long have they been a director of the company?

⇨ In what other companies have they been (or are currently) directors or senior executives?

⇨ What's their track record? How successful were the companies that they were associated with at senior executive level?

If you become a shareholder, you'll be invited to attend the annual general meeting and then you'll be able to form a first-hand opinion of the directors.

Chapter summary

⇨ For a long-term share portfolio it's safest to invest primarily in shares with good fundamentals.

⇨ The shares should be fully paid ordinary shares listed on the ASX.

⇨ Generally speaking, it's best to invest in companies that operate primarily in Australia.

⇨ The shares you consider should be highly liquid; that is, they should have a significant trading volume each day.

⇨ The shares you consider should trade at a relatively high price, one that's in dollars rather than cents.

⇨ Companies should have a high market capitalisation, with the total value of shares issued being several hundreds of millions or billions of dollars.

⇨ Companies should make a good profit and have done so for a significant period of time.

⇨ Companies should pay a reasonable dividend that's preferably fully franked.

⇨ Debt levels should be reasonable; the debt to equity ratio shouldn't be excessively high, the interest cover should be comfortable and the current ratio should be greater than 1.0.

⇨ There should be a stable and reputable board of directors and competent senior executives.

⇨ It's difficult to measure directorship objectively, but you can easily research the members of the board and senior executives and their qualifications and track record.

⇨ It can be dangerous to invest in a company simply because there's a good product for which there's a growing demand. A business with a good product won't necessarily be a profitable one or prove to be a good investment if other important criteria for success aren't met.

chapter 9

Trading shares at the right price

In chapter 8 I looked at the fundamentals of shares you should consider for a long-term portfolio. These fundamentals didn't include price considerations. You might want to buy some shares that fulfil your fundamental criteria but you need to buy them at a good price. In this chapter I'll discuss relevant price factors you need to think about if you're considering trading shares.

Relationship between share price and earnings

For a listed company the most important factor that drives the share price is profitability, also known as earnings. The important profit statistic for shares is the earnings per share (EPS), and it's normally expressed in cents per ordinary share. Almost always there's a very strong correlation between share price and earnings per share, as I've illustrated in figure 9.1 (overleaf).

Figure 9.1: relationship between share price and earnings

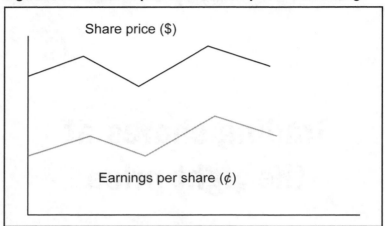

As you can see, it's generally the case that when earnings increase the share price rises and when the earnings decrease the share price falls. However, the correlation is not usually an exact one. In particular the market doesn't like earnings downgrades, and these often cause a greater corresponding fall in price than would seem justified. For example, an earnings downgrade of 10% might result in a 15% or 20% fall in the share price.

You don't need to be a rocket scientist to work out why share price and EPS are so strongly correlated. If you were going to buy a business, the most important factor is how much profit you could expect per dollar of capital you're investing in the business. As discussed in chapter 8, the bottom line with any company is how much profit it's making and whether those earnings can be sustained into the future. Shareholders are the owners of the business and they look closely at the EPS when setting the market price of shares.

Price to earnings ratio

There's a statistic that helps you to relate the share price and the EPS: the price to earnings ratio (PE). (In some financial listings PE is shown as P/E or PER but I'll use PE). The price to earnings ratio is calculated by dividing the share price by the EPS. The mathematical formula is:

$$PE = \frac{\text{Share price (cents)}}{\text{Earnings per share (cents)}}$$

Because EPS is given in cents per share, when calculating PE the share price needs to be shown in cents. The earnings per share is calculated using the published (or announced) earnings for the year to date divided by the number of shares on issue. It's important to note that a company's earnings statistics are usually published only every six months and that there could be a two-month delay between the end of the period and the finalisation of the financial statistics. Therefore the published EPS for the year to date will be up to date for a period that's between two and eight months backward in time.

Example 1
The price of a share is $2.25 and the EPS is 15¢. What's the PE?

Solution
First convert the share price of $2.25 to cents by multiplying by 100.

$2.25 \times 100 = 225$¢
PE = 225 ÷ 15 = **15**

In share table listings you're usually given the PE and the share price but the EPS may not be shown. If you want to work it out, you divide the share price by the PE.

Example 2
If the share price of Commonwealth Bank is $52.50 and the PE is 16, what's the EPS?

Solution
Firstly, you need to convert the share price in dollars to cents by multiplying by 100 (as in example 1).

$52.50 × 100 = 5250¢
EPS = Price ÷ PE = 5250 ÷ 16 = 328 (cents per share)

That is, the EPS is **$3.28**. (As is customary in financial listings, I rounded down the EPS figure to three digits.)

If the company isn't making a profit (operating at a loss), earnings are negative. Therefore the EPS is negative and PE is negative. However, in most financial listings negative PEs aren't shown and the PE column is left blank.

Tip
A quick and easy way of checking whether a listed company is making a profit is to look at the PE column in financial listings. If it's blank or shown as a dash then you know that the company is operating at a loss.

Effect of share price on PE

If there's no change in the published earnings per share, what happens to the PE as trades take place in the market and the share price changes? The effect is as follows:

⇨ An increase in the share price results in a rise in the PE.

⇨ A decrease in the share price results in a fall in the PE.

The change to the PE is in the same proportion as the change in the EPS. If the price changes (up or down) by 5%, the PE will also change by 5%.

Reasonable share price

When you shop for any commodity, whether food, clothing, whitegoods, computers or whatever, you usually compare prices and try to buy at the lowest price possible. This mindset doesn't really work with shares as price isn't a good indication of value. You need to shift your focus from price alone to price in conjunction with earnings. That's why the price to earnings ratio is so important: it relates price to earnings in a single statistic. So the question that now arises is: how can you use the PE to decide whether or not a share price is reasonable?

Clearly, if no PE is shown the company isn't making a profit and you're in no-man's-land (or no-woman's-land). That's not the type of company you want in your portfolio, so this situation isn't one you need to consider. For all companies making a profit, one way you can evaluate the 'fairness' of a share price is by comparing the PE of the company to the average market PE.

Average market PE

In Australia, for companies that are making a profit the average PE has historically been around 16 to 17. I'll show you how to use this knowledge to evaluate the 'fairness' of the share price in example 3.

Tip

It the average sharemarket PE rises significantly above the long-term average, beware! It's a sign that the market is overheated and that a correction (downturn) will occur. On the other hand, if the average market PE is significantly below the long-term average it's a sign of over-correction resulting from undue pessimism and it's a good indication that a market rise will occur.

Example 3
Evaluate the fairness of the share price of the following three companies, by comparing their PE to the average market PE of 16 to 17.

Company	Share price	PE
A	$1.42	22.4
B	$16.70	8.7
C	$6.48	16.3

Solution

By looking at the PEs you can conclude that:

Company A is **overpriced (expensive)**
Company B is **underpriced (cheap)**
Company C is **about right**

You can see from this simple example that the share price itself gives you no real indication of price value. If you'd compared the share prices only, no doubt you'd have said that Company B's shares were the most expensive and Company A's were the cheapest. That's not the case at all when price is related to earnings, and is a false conclusion.

Tip

With shares, price is misleading as it doesn't give you a good indication of value for money. A better indicator is the PE, and often the highest priced shares are actually the cheapest in terms of value based upon earnings. In the same way, the lowest priced shares are often the most costly in terms of earnings value.

Taking future profits into account

When you look at share listings you'll see that some shares have PEs well above average (indicating that they're overpriced) and some have PEs well below average (underpriced). Why are investors prepared to pay a great deal more for some shares than can be justified by the earnings and pay a great deal less for others?

The main reason is that listed PEs are based on *past* earnings. As discussed in chapter 8, past profits reinvested help to build a sound company, but nevertheless share prices are based more upon market perceptions about *future* performance than historical performance. As a share investor you can easily get a fix on past earnings from published financial data and by looking at PE ratios and comparing them to the market average. But how can you take future profits into account when evaluating the fairness of a share price?

Fortunately there's a published statistic that helps you assess share price value based upon future profits: the price to earnings growth ratio (I'll abbreviate it to PEG). It's calculated in the following way:

$$PEG = \frac{PE}{EGP}$$

Where:

PE = Current PE

EGP = Forecast earnings per share growth next year
expressed as a percentage

PEG is based upon current PE—that is, *current* market price but *past* earnings per share (year to date earnings)—whereas EGP is based upon forecast future earnings per share growth for *next year*. If next year's earnings are expected to be below this year's, then the earnings growth will be negative. Negative PEGs aren't usually shown in financial listings and the PEG statistic is shown as a blank space or a dash.

Example 4

In published statistics the following information about a share is given:

Last sale price = $1.60
Earnings per share = 10¢ (based on year-to-date earnings)
Forecast earnings per share = 12¢ (based on next year's
expected earnings)

Determine the PE and the PEG.

Solution

In order to calculate PE, as before it's necessary to convert the share price into cents.

$1.60 = 160¢

PE = 160 ÷ 10 = **16**

The earnings growth percentage is calculated as follows:

Earnings growth = 12 – 10 = 2¢ per share
Earnings growth fraction = 2 ÷ 10 = 0.2

To convert to a percentage, multiply by 100:

0.2 × 100 = 20%
Therefore EGP = 20

That is, the earnings per share is forecast to grow by 20% next year.

Now calculate the PEG, as follows:

PEG = PE ÷ EGP = 16 ÷ 20 = **0.8**

You generally won't need to do this calculation yourself as the PE and PEG are often shown in financial statistics data. However, if you can do the number crunching yourself you're better able to get a grip on the real meaning of the statistics.

Tip

PE is a very common financial statistic shown in most published share listings. PEG is not so commonly published and you may need to delve a little deeper to find it. I'll show you how to do this in chapter 12.

Using PEG to determine value

The question that now needs to be answered is: 'what's a fair share price based upon the PEG?'

There's no hard and fast criteria but there's a rule of thumb you can use. This says that PEG = 1 represents fair value. This rule indicates that the price of a share is justified when the price to earnings ratio is the same as the expected percentage growth in earnings. I'll show you how this works in the following example.

Example 5

Use the PEG rule to work out what growth in earnings is necessary to justify the price of shares A, B and C with the following PEs:

A = 5
B = 15
C = 25

Solution

Using the PEG rule, the PE should be the same as the expected growth in earnings. Therefore the necessary earnings growth of each share is as follows:

A = **5%**
B = **15%**
C = **25%**

You can see that the PEG indicates that the higher the PE the greater the earnings growth needed to justify the share price. In other words, shares with high PEs are those where investors perceive high potential growth in earnings. Also the rule indicates that shares with low PEs that seem undervalued are those where investors perceive little earnings growth potential.

Overpriced and underpriced shares based on PEG

The PEG allows you to draw the following conclusions about share price value:

Fair value: PEG = 1
Overpriced: PEG > 1
Underpriced: PEG < 1

Expensive (overpriced) shares are those where the share price can't be justified by the expected growth in earnings. These are shares where investor enthusiasm has pushed prices beyond what can be justified by forecast earnings growth—there's a fair amount of blue sky potential built into the price. Bargain (underpriced) shares are those that investors aren't enthusiastic about as they don't see the potential for earnings growth.

The share given in example 4 is an example of an under-priced share because the PEG < 1.

Tip

Beware of shares that have high PEGs unless you believe the blue sky potential built into the price can be justified. Also beware of shares that have low PEGs; bargains can be found in the sharemarket, but they're rare.

Example 6

Work out what share price and PE you can expect next year for the share from example 4 given the following information:

> Last sale price = $1.60
> Current EPS = 10¢
> PE = 16
> Forecast EPS = 12¢
> PEG = 0.8
> EGP = 20

Solution

As I've previously said (and illustrated in figure 9.1), it's most likely that the share price will rise in the same proportion as the earnings per share. The current price is $1.60 and 20% of this is $0.32.

Therefore next year's price should be:

$1.60 + $0.32 = **$1.92**

So next year's PE would be:

$$192 \div 12 = \mathbf{16}$$

The PE remains the same because the price can be expected to change by the same percentage as the growth in earnings.

Earnings forecasts

By now, you're probably pondering the question: 'where do the earnings forecasts come from and how reliable are they?'

As an investor you'd like to think that earnings forecasts would come from the most knowledgeable source available; that is, from the company directors. However, that's not the usual scenario and directors are usually reluctant to quantify future earnings expectations. It's far more common for directors to use qualitative rather than quantitative terms when describing future profit expectations. For example, in annual reports you'll generally find statements such as:

⇨ 'Due to the difficult trading conditions we're currently experiencing, earnings were below expectations. However, your directors are making every effort to improve profitability and the measures we've put in place can be expected to bear fruit in the future.'

⇨ 'Next year we expect earnings to be maintained at current levels.'

⇨ 'Your directors are confident that earnings will continue to grow in line with expectations.'

These types of statements can't be used to calculate expected earnings per share. So published earnings forecasts are obtained from other sources—generally from one or more financial analysts who provide the information that data providers publish. Naturally no-one can predict the future, and therefore there's always a fair degree of uncertainty associated with earnings forecasts. As an investor you can't do anything about this; the best you can do is work the probabilities in your favour by taking the published information at face value and assuming it's the best estimate available. You can modify the data if you disagree with the analyst's estimates but you need good reasons for doing so.

Tip

Published data regarding future earnings expectations is generally the most reliable guide available.

Extended forecasts

As well as accessing next year's forecasts, it's often possible to access forecasts beyond next year. How can you use these extended forecasts to determine share price value?

Clearly you can use these forecasts to extend your PEG analysis further into the future. However, I seldom do this as I believe it's difficult enough to obtain reliable earnings forecasts for next year, let alone for years further into the future. So I don't place a great deal of faith in extended forecasts and use them only as a guide to longer term earnings growth.

Tip

You can use extended forecasts as a guide to longer term performance but don't rely on them.

Chapter summary

⇨ Even though you're investing for the long term, it's important to buy shares at a good price and not at a price that can't be justified by earnings.

⇨ Share prices will generally move in the same way as the expected earnings per share.

⇨ Investors often punish earnings downgrades more than is justified by the expected fall in EPS. This may present a good buying opportunity.

⇨ The PE ratio is a good guide to value and it's calculated by dividing the share price (in cents) by the earnings per share (in cents).

⇨ It's generally best to avoid buying shares that have a PE greatly above (or below) the market average.

⇨ Over a long period, the market average PE in Australia has been in the range 16 to 17.

⇨ Shares with a PE well above the market average are inherently more risky as there's a fair amount of blue sky potential built into the price.

⇨ When average market PE rises much above the long-term average you can expect a market correction downward some time in the future.

⇨ When the average market PE falls much below the long-term average you can expect a market move upward some time in the future.

⇨ Published PEs are based upon *current* share prices (generally at close of trade each day) but *past* earnings (year to date). Therefore the PE really is a historical value and not a guide to the future.

⇨ If the earnings don't change, a change in the share price results in a corresponding change in the PE.

⇨ In order to get a fix on the future you can use the price to earnings growth ratio (PEG).

⇨ The PEG is calculated by dividing the PE by the expected percentage growth in earnings per share.

⇨ PEG = 1 represents fair value, whereas PEG > 1 indicates a share price that's too high and can't be justified based upon earnings expectations. PEG < 1 indicates a share price that's too low based upon earnings expectations and a share that's been unduly punished by investors.

⇨ Extended forecasts of earnings beyond next year are often published but shouldn't be taken too seriously because of the high degree of uncertainty associated with them.

chapter 10

Trading shares at the right time

In this chapter I'll consider the timing of your trades; that is, the right time to buy (or sell). This is an area of share investing that's known as technical analysis (because this method is based upon charts it's also known as charting).

Why consider timing?

There's a stock market saying:

> It's not timing the market but time in the market that's important.

If that's so, then for long-term share investing why do you need to consider timing? Surely if you're trading at the right price that must automatically be the right time.

To answer this question, consider the scenario outlined in the following example.

Example 1

You're interested in some shares because their fundamentals are attractive. However, they're overpriced with a high PE so you decide not to buy but keep an eye on them. In time the price falls and the PE falls correspondingly. When the price falls to a level where the PE is more reasonable you decide to act and buy some shares. You congratulate yourself for being smart and waiting to buy at a better price.

However, your gratification turns to chagrin when the price continues to fall and within a few weeks is considerably lower than your purchase price. You're making an appreciable capital loss on your purchase, and it takes a long time before the price recovers to your purchase price and you start to show a capital gain on the shares.

Conclusion

What went wrong? This scenario is, I suspect, a rather common one and illustrates the importance of timing. Even though you bought the shares at a reasonable price, you bought them at the wrong time.

The right time to buy

There are three possible outcomes as share trades take place in the market:

⇨ the price rises

⇨ the price remains reasonably steady

⇨ the price falls.

Clearly, after you've bought shares you'd like the price to rise so you make a capital gain; that's the most desirable outcome. If the price remains reasonably steady, that's okay in the short term provided the price doesn't track down in the longer term. If the price falls after purchase, that's the most undesirable outcome and one you're trying to avoid.

So the right time to buy is when the price is rising and the worst time to buy is when the price is falling. So the question is: how do you know if you're buying at the right time?

There's no foolproof answer to this question, but you can work the probabilities in your favour. I'll now outline how you can do so.

Trading with the trend

The best way to play the probabilities is to trade with the trend. That's because share prices generally have a characteristic known as momentum. Simply put, this means that when the share price moves in one particular direction over a period of time, the move gathers momentum and is more likely to continue than to change direction. Indeed, it usually takes some major event to cause a change in momentum.

When a share price moves in a certain direction for an extended period this is known as a trend. There are three possible trends:

⇨ uptrend: the price moves up over an extended period

⇨ directionless (or sideways trend): the price hovers around the same level for an extended period

⇨ downtrend: the price moves down over an extended period.

You're working the probabilities in your favour if you trade with the trend. There's a sharemarket principle that's worth remembering:

The trend is your friend.

Tip

While you can sometimes make good profits being a contrarian, it's generally safer to trade in the direction of an established trend.

Buying shares with the trend

Following the trend principle, if you want to buy shares it's best to buy in an uptrend. I try to avoid using words like 'always' or 'never' because on the sharemarket exceptions to any principle (or rule) often occur—even the best ones. But one time I might use the word 'never' is to say: never buy in a downtrend. It's usually disastrous to do so. I once outlined this principle in a share investing course, and about two years afterward I met one of the participants. He told me that just by applying this one principle to his share purchases he had avoided disasters and had made heaps of extra profit.

Buying in a sideways trend is okay if the price eventually moves up and out of this trend after you've bought, but not if the share price moves down instead. It's impossible to predict which way the price will move out of a well-established sideways trend, so it's more risky to buy in such a trend and it's better to delay until a breakout occurs (if in fact it does). If there's an upward breakout, then fine, now's the time to buy. You won't be buying at the best price but you're taking less risk.

Tip
Buy in an uptrend, wait in a sideways trend and never buy in a downtrend.

Selling shares with the trend

If you want to sell shares, if you follow the trend principle you should adopt the reverse procedure; that is, sell in a downtrend, wait in a sideways trend and don't sell in an uptrend. However, there are variations you might wish to consider:

⇨ Frequently a sideways trend can remain over long periods because something dramatic is needed to shake the price out of the lethargic state it's in. So if you want to sell, it may be a good idea to sell in a sideways trend rather than to wait until a trend change occurs.

⇨ Some traders follow the principle of cashing in profits and sell if the price rises to a point where the trade is a profitable one. Indeed, there's another sharemarket saying:

You can't go broke by cashing in profits.

Certainly, it's not disastrous to sell in an uptrend if you're making good profits but it's not a principle I use or recommend. After all, why not make more profit if you can? Some people call this greed but I think that's a silly way of looking at it; rather I believe it's simply being astute. Let's face it, some shares you buy may turn out to be losers so you need some good wins to more than compensate for any losses. You have to be very lucky to pick the exact top of an uptrend, and if the price is trending upward it is more likely to continue in that direction than to suddenly reverse. So why not make some extra profit if you can? If the uptrend does reverse, that's the time to sell and take profits.

Tip

Sell in a downtrend, sell (or wait) in a sideways trend and don't sell in an uptrend.

We can now look at example 1 again and pinpoint the problem. I hope you've spotted it. Even though the price looked good, you bought in a downtrend. You should have waited until the price bottomed and started to reverse and move upward before you bought.

Tip

When a share price has fallen from previously high levels, don't get too excited and trade quickly in order to get a 'bargain price'. By exercising restraint, you may not buy at the best price but you minimise the risk of a loss that you'd regret later on.

Example 2

Let's now look at the share price chart in figure 10.1. This chart is a one-year line chart of daily closing prices for ANZ Bank and it's typical of the type of chart you can expect with most shares.

Figure 10.1: ANZ price chart

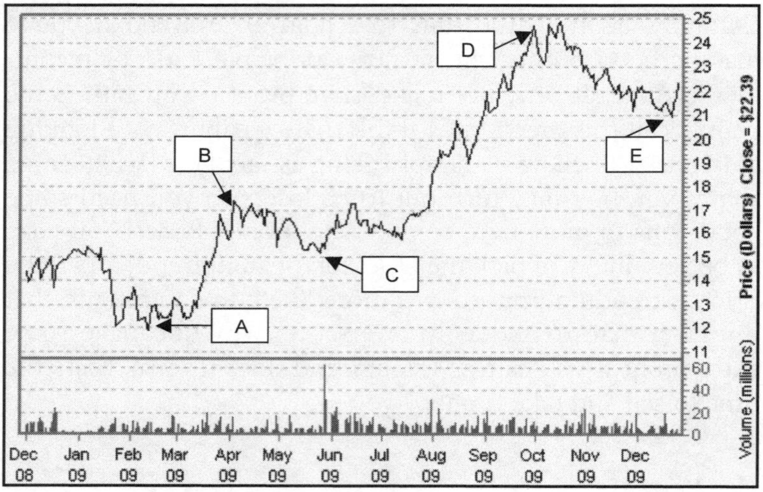

Source: www.CommSec.com.au / Wall St on Demand

(This chart was created using the charting facility on the CommSec site. Recently, the charting facility has been updated so its charts now have a somewhat different format. However, the basic price line is not affected by the change.)

When you look at this chart, it's easy to be clever using the wisdom of hindsight. You might say: 'I could have bought at point A for about $12 and sold at point B for around $17 and made a good profit of $5 per share (about 42%) in only a few months. Later I could have bought again at point C for around $15 and sold again at point D for around $24.50 and made a further profit of $9.50 per share (about 63%) in only four months or so'.

Great isn't it — except there's a catch. You can't buy shares retrospectively and you can't use the wisdom of hindsight to make profits. If you look at figure 10.1 again, you can see that had you bought shares at point D for around $24.00 while the price was falling you'd be making a capital loss at the present time (end of the chart period) as the price tracked down to point E before recovering.

Conclusion

You can't make profitable trades retrospectively using the wisdom of hindsight. You can only trade today on the basis of the most likely future scenario.

Support and resistance levels

In a sideways trend, as shares are traded the price never remains exactly the same but fluctuates up and down as time goes on. If the sideways trend takes place over a reasonable time period, the price often bounces around between high and low values. The low value is known as the support level and the high value is known as the resistance level. These names are descriptive because they indicate market sentiment. When the price reaches the support level, the market perceives that the shares are good value and there's buying pressure to drive the price up. When the price reaches the resistance level, the market perceives that the shares are fully priced and there's selling pressure as traders cash in profits. This cycle can repeat over a considerable time period, and is illustrated in figure 10.2.

Figure 10.2: support and resistance levels

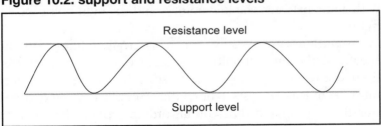

Sometimes the price will overshoot or undershoot the levels briefly but that doesn't alter the basic concept of price support and resistance.

Tip

A sustained price breakout above a resistance level is usually significant and indicates an optimistic change in trader sentiment and is often a good time to buy. A sustained price breakout below a support level is also significant and indicates a pessimistic change in trader sentiment and is a good time to stay away (or sell).

Identifying trends

Identification and analysis of trends is the main purpose of technical analysis. Over the years many ways of identifying trends have been developed, but in the interests of simplicity I'll outline only two: the eyeball method and the moving average method.

The eyeball method

As the name suggests, you use this method when you try to identify trends by examining a chart and using your own judgement to see what trends appear evident. As an example, consider the price chart for Commonwealth Bank (CBA) in figure 10.3.

I think you'll agree that rocket science isn't needed to identify a big uptrend on this chart. I'll draw this uptrend with a line between the low point A and the high point F (see figure 10.4).

Trendlines are usually drawn as straight lines. Strictly speaking, the lines should be straight only if the chart has been drawn using a logarithmic scale for prices. However, most technical analysts ignore this complication and draw trendlines as straight lines on an ordinary price chart where prices are drawn on a linear scale.

Figure 10.3: CBA price chart

Source: www.CommSec.com.au / Wall St on Demand

Figure 10.4: CBA price chart with uptrend shown (A–F)

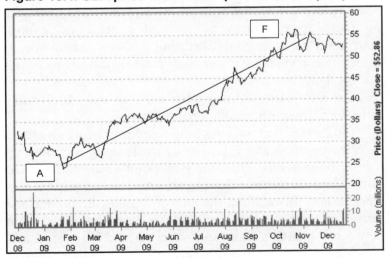

Source: www.CommSec.com.au / Wall St on Demand

When identifying trends you should really draw the chart as a bar chart, OHLC (open, high, low, close) chart or candle chart, and draw uptrend lines through the daily low points and downtrend lines through the daily high points. This is another complication that I'm going to ignore in the interests of simplicity; I've used a line chart showing closing prices only and drawn the trendline as a line of approximate best fit.

Early trend identification

Unless you've perfected a time machine and can project yourself backward in time, looking at a historical share price chart and working out what you *could have done* isn't going to help you build your wealth in the future. To make good capital gains from shares, you need to be able to detect an uptrend early enough to be able to get onboard the trend and buy at a good price, before the price rises too high or the trend runs out of steam. If you're holding shares and a downtrend reversal occurs, you may want to jump ship before you suffer substantial losses. The eyeball method is useful once a long-term trend becomes established, but it may not help you to detect a trend change early enough to allow you to buy or sell at a good price.

Let's look at the CBA price chart again in figure 10.5 — this time I've marked some additional points.

You can see that the long-term trend previously identified between points A and F is actually made up of a number of shorter term trends. From the start point at the extreme left of the chart there was a downtrend until the low point A was reached and this marked the end of the downtrend and the start of an uptrend to B. Then there's a short downtrend again between B and C, a short and steep uptrend between C and D, a longer sideways trend between D and E, a long uptrend between E and F and finally a sideways trend or perhaps a shallow downtrend between F and G.

Figure 10.5: CBA price chart with short-term trends

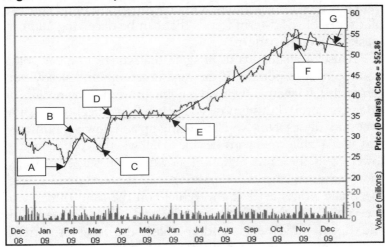

Source: www.CommSec.com.au / Wall St on Demand

If during this period you were thinking of buying CBA shares, how would you have known to buy at point A? And how would you have known not to sell at point B when a shorter term downtrend appeared only to be quickly replaced by a steep uptrend? Even if you had bought at point A, would you've been tempted to sell after point D when the sideways trend continued, reasoning that the uptrend was over and the price wouldn't rise further?

And more importantly, at the current time on the chart (point G), what do you think will happen in the future? If you're holding CBA shares, will you sell, reasoning that the good uptrend is over and that the price is now going nowhere? Or do you think that between F and G it's just a pause as occurred between D and E previously, and that now's a good time to buy more before the price takes off again?

Price fluctuations

The CBA chart I've used is typical of the type of chart you'll find with most shares. It's seldom the case that a long-term trend takes place in a smooth manner with prices moving in the same direction each day. Rather, a long-term trend consists of a series of short-term trends that can be deceiving and can mask the overall pattern.

A useful analogy is to imagine that you're in a car going from point A to point B. If the road is smooth and steady, you can easily tell whether the road is going upwards, downwards or sideways (level). But suppose you're in a four-wheel-drive going over sand dunes. Now you'll be going up and down continually, and after a while you won't be able to tell whether you're higher, lower or at the same elevation as when you started. Clearly, short-term movements are masking the long-term trend.

Share prices act like the vehicle on the sand dunes, not the vehicle on the smooth, steady road. The short-term up and down movements tend to mask the long-term trend and can make trend identification difficult using the eyeball method alone. Fortunately, there's a charting aid that helps you to differentiate between short-term fluctuations and long-term trends. It's known as the moving average.

Moving averages

To understand the principle of moving averages consider the following question. There are two populations of people and you want to know if there's any difference in height between them. Clearly, it wouldn't help much measuring a few people from each population because of individual differences. It's necessary to measure a fairly large sample from each population and calculate the average height. The average amalgamates individual differences and provides better overall differentiation.

In the same way, because share prices fluctuate from day to day, comparing one day to another doesn't help much when you're trying to identify a trend. You need to average the price over a number of days and see if the average is moving up or down. If the average is moving up you can be more confident of an uptrend, and if it's moving down you can be more confident of a downtrend. If it's remaining about the same, then you can be fairly confident of a sideways trend.

Tip

Use moving averages to be more confident of trends.

Types of moving average

There are a number of different moving averages that are calculated differently. The two most common are the simple moving average and the exponential moving average. There's also another one known as the weighted moving average but it's not frequently used.

The simple moving average (SMA) is just an ordinary average where the prices are added together and then the sum is divided by the number of days in the calculation.

The exponential moving average (EMA) is calculated in such a way as to give more weight to recent prices than to prices going back further in time. (I won't outline the calculation method as it's rather complex.)

Most charting packages allow you to use either one, so after you've become familiar with using moving averages you can experiment and decide on your preference. The claimed advantage of the EMA is that the average is more sensitive to recent trend changes, but I've found no significant advantage in using the EMA rather than the SMA.

Tip

Use the SMA as a charting aid to detect trends, but experiment with the EMA as well and decide on your preference.

Long-term trend identification using a moving average

To see how a moving average helps you to better identify trends, I've taken the chart for CBA and superimposed a 30-day SMA on it (figure 10.6, overleaf).

Figure 10.6: CBA price chart with 30-day SMA

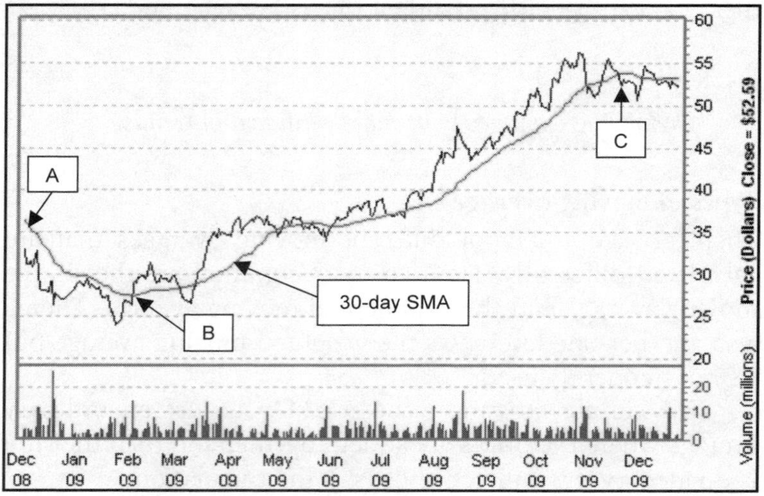

Source: www.CommSec.com.au / Wall St on Demand

You can see how the moving average has smoothed the short-term price fluctuations and simplified trend identification. Clearly, there's a downtrend between A and B and an uptrend between B and C. So if you'd based your trading decision on the moving average, you wouldn't have bought the shares until some time after point B and you'd have held them all the way up to point C. The moving average indicates that from point C until the end of the chart, the shares have taken a breather and the price is moving sideways.

Charting time periods

Most charting packages allow you to vary the time period over which the chart is drawn and the time period used for calculating the moving average. So the question arises: over what time period should you draw the chart and what time period should you specify for calculating the moving average?

There's no simple answer to this question, but my suggestion is that as an investor (not a day trader) you adopt the following approach:

⇨ Use a five-year chart with a moving average in the range 50 to 70 days. This chart will give you a good idea of the longer term trends.

⇨ Then use a one-year chart with a moving average of 30 days or so. This chart will give you a good idea of more recent trends or trend changes.

In figure 10.6 I've already shown a one-year chart with a 30-day moving average for CBA. To give you an idea of what a five-year chart looks like, I have included one for CBA in figure 10.7.

Figure 10.7: five-year CBA price chart with 50-day SMA

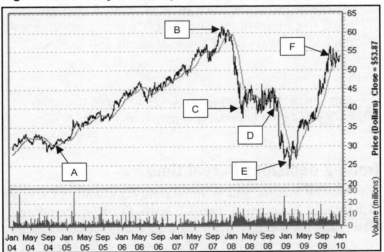

Source: www.CommSec.com.au / Wall St on Demand

From this chart I've drawn the following conclusions:

⇨ In 2004 the price didn't do much, cresting a bit and then falling slightly to a low point at A of about $30.

⇨ From the low point (A), it started a long uptrend with the moving average tracking steadily upward. This trend lasted for about three years to point B, where the shares hit a high value of about $60.

⇨ This long uptrend was followed by a fairly rapid downtrend to point C, where the shares dropped to a low of about $40.

⇨ Then followed a sideways trend for about a year, with the SMA basically flat and with the price ranging between a support of about $40 and resistance of about $45. Then at around the end of 2008 at point D, as the global financial crisis took hold, the priced dropped rapidly to a low at point E of about $25.

⇨ As the panic subsided, the price recovered and the SMA changed direction. A fairly steady uptrend was established to point F at a price of about $55. Then the trend lost momentum, and the price took a breather and tracked sideways in the range of about $50 to $55.

Tip

A long-term price chart with a long-term moving average gives you a good impression of long-term trends.

Trading decisions in real time

Suppose the present time is at the right-hand end of the chart in figure 10.7, and you own CBA shares or you're contemplating buying some. What should you do? Does the charting evidence indicate that you should buy, sell, wait or hold? How do you make trading decisions in real time?

I suggest that from the charting analysis you could reasonably come to the following conclusions:

⇨ Point F in the five-year chart looks rather like the pattern after point C and suggests that the price will remain in a sideways trend, having support at about the $50 level and resistance at about the $55 level.

⇨ If you already own CBA shares, hold. There's no reason to sell; the price is moving sideways and you'll still be making a good profit from the dividends.

⇨ If you're thinking of buying CBA shares, it would be prudent to wait until the moving average starts to move up again. However, if you want the dividend yield, you could buy at a short-term low point as it seems unlikely that there will be a significant price downturn in the near future. We know that the previous sudden drop after the sideways trend was due to the global financial crisis, and as the crisis appears to be over there seems little downside risk at present price levels.

Tip

It's a good idea to study a chart and try to find an explanation for any unexpected trend changes. You're then in a better position to make a reasonable prediction of whether or not history is likely to repeat itself.

Multiple moving averages

Many charting packages allow you to place more than one moving average on a chart. It's common to have two moving averages; you can use a shorter moving average as well as a longer one. For example, you could use a shorter moving average in the range 15 to 30 days and a longer one in the range 50 to 150 days. The shorter moving average detects trend changes faster than the longer one, whereas the longer one provides better smoothing of day-to-day price fluctuations and allows you to more readily see the longer term trends. Clearly, a chart showing two moving averages as well as daily prices gives you heaps of information in one chart. Figure 10.8 (overleaf) shows an example of such a chart with two moving averages. It's a five-year chart for CBA with a 30-day and a 100-day SMA.

Figure 10.8: CBA chart with a 30-day and a 100-day SMA

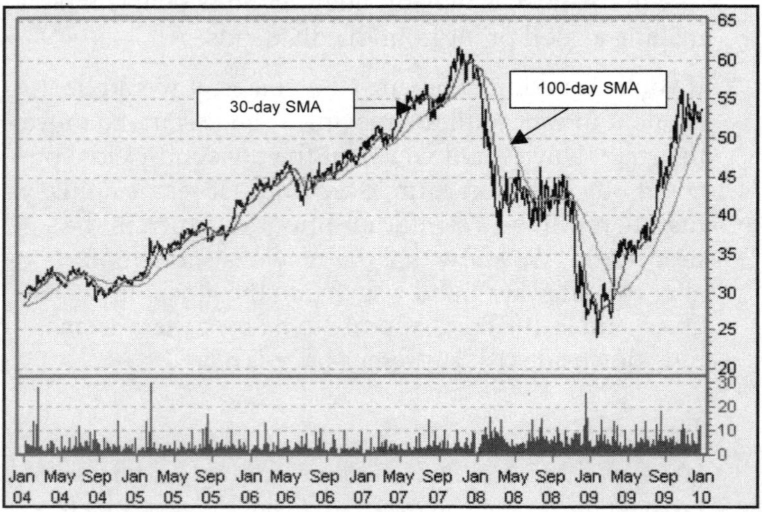

Source: www.CommSec.com.au / Wall St on Demand

You can see from this chart that the 30-day SMA closely follows the price action whereas the 100-day SMA smooths out a lot of this action and gives a much clearer impression of the long-term trend.

Tip

As you become more familiar with moving averages and their significance, use charts with two moving averages drawn simultaneously: a shorter term and a longer term one. Experiment with the moving average time periods and note the effect of changing them.

Improving your technical analysis skills

One of the great benefits of computers and charting packages available on the internet is you can practise and experiment without any cost or detriment. So why not take advantage of this to improve your trading skills? I suggest you obtain charts for several different stocks, identify trends on them and then forecast what you think may take place in the future. Some time later, update and review the charts to see whether your forecasts were correct. If not, try to identify if there was any flaw in your analysis or if there was some cause for the change that no-one could have reasonably predicted. If there was a flaw in your analysis, investigate it and try to discover how you could be more accurate in the future. You can't be right all the time, but if you can make more correct decisions than incorrect ones you're well on the way to proficiency with technical analysis. Also experiment with chart formats, time periods and so on to see what effect varying these has on the accuracy of your forecasts.

Daily price rises and falls of relatively small magnitude always take place with the day-to-day trades on the share-market. Twice a year when shares go ex-dividend there's generally a price fall at least equal to the amount of the dividend. These changes are perfectly normal and part and parcel of share trading, and are not of any significance to the longer term trend. However, when a long-term trend changes direction it is significant and there's always a cause. When this occurs, it's very important to try to identify the causes of the trend change. You can do this by looking for any company announcements or press releases that could explain the change. I discuss this in greater detail in chapter 14.

Tip

Hone your technical analysis skills by experimenting. When a long-term trend change occurs, try to identify the cause.

Technical analysis tools and filters

Technical analysis is a complex and comprehensive area of analysis that requires a great deal of study and many years of experience in order to become an expert in it. There are many other tools (also known as filters) in the technical analysis toolkit available with many charting packages that I haven't discussed. At least 50 different tools and indicators have been developed, including MACD (moving average convergence divergence), RSI (relative strength index), momentum, on balance volume and money flow indicators—just to mention a few. I've outlined the basic principles to enable you to identify trends and trend changes and minimise the likelihood of buying or selling shares at the wrong time. The good news is that I've seen no evidence to indicate that a complex system using many tools and filters works all the time, or indeed produces better results in the long run than a simple system using only a few. However, should you want to delve deeper into technical analysis I suggest you refer to either of my other two books: *Teach Yourself about Shares* or *Online Investing on the Australian Sharemarket*. Also there are many other dedicated books and websites that can provide further information.

Chapter summary

⇨ As well as trading shares at the right price, it's important to buy or sell at the right time.

⇨ Buy in an uptrend and don't buy in a downtrend.

⇨ Sell in a downtrend and don't sell in an uptrend.

⇨ Wait for trend confirmation before trading. You won't get the best price but you'll reduce the risk of loss.

⇨ Exercise restraint with your trading decisions and try to avoid acting impulsively.

⇨ The 'eyeball' method can be used to detect trends and trend changes but is best used in conjunction with moving averages.

⇨ A moving average smooths out the day-to-day price fluctuations. The longer the term of the moving average, the greater the amount of smoothing.

⇨ In a sideways trend, support and resistance levels can usually be identified. A sustained breakout above a resistance level or below a support level usually indicates a change in market sentiment and a significant trend change.

⇨ In order to detect long-term trends use a relatively long-term chart with a relatively long-term moving average. To detect the latest action and trend changes use a relatively short-term chart and a relatively short-term moving average.

⇨ Most charting packages allow you to use two moving averages simultaneously. For maximum information and visual impact, use both a longer and a shorter term moving average with a longer term (5 to 10 years) and a shorter term (six months to one year) chart.

⇨ When a long-term trend change occurs in a chart, there's always a reason. Try to find out what that reason was by checking if there were any announcements or press releases around the time of the change that could explain it.

⇨ History often repeats itself, and past trend changes can recur in the future if a similar situation arises again. By identifying these, you can make better trading decisions in real time.

⇨ Most charting packages allow you to vary the chart time periods and moving average time periods. Experiment with charts drawn over different time periods and with different moving average time periods and decide which ones you prefer.

⇨ Experiment with charting and by doing so develop your technical analysis acumen.

chapter 11

Setting up to trade

In this chapter I outline how you can set yourself up so you can trade shares; that is, buy and sell them. If you've had experience trading shares and are completely satisfied with the service provided by your broker, you need only skim through this chapter.

Trading shares outside the ASX trading facility

Like any other tradeable commodity, share ownership can be transferred via a contract between two parties. Shares can be traded without using the ASX trading facility. This can take place in two different ways that I'll now briefly outline.

Trading by agreement

If you find someone who wants to buy shares you own or sell you shares, this can be legally arranged without using the ASX trading facility or the services of an agent. However, this is uncommon, except when very large and valuable parcels of shares are traded; for example, with company directors or financial institutions. In such instances this method is used to minimise trading costs.

Transfer of share ownership without trading

Share ownership can also be transferred from one party to another without a trade. For example, if you want to set up a self managed superannuation fund or a family/testamentary trust you can transfer shares you own into the fund or trust without trading them. If you do transfer shares privately you'll need to fill out a transfer of ownership form and advise the share registry. Legally, it will be regarded as a trade and will invoke capital gains tax obligations.

Another common situation where transfer of ownership occurs without trading is upon the death of a shareowner who has bequeathed shares to a beneficiary in his or her will. In this case, no capital gains tax obligations are invoked until such time as a beneficiary decides to sell the shares. Then capital gains will be based upon the original purchase cost and not the value of the shares at the time of transfer.

Tip

Accrued capital losses can't be transferred to a beneficiary. If you have any such losses and you're getting on in life, it can be a good idea to offset them by selling some profitable shares. Then the taxation benefit of the loss won't go down the gurgler.

Trading shares using the ASX trading facility

By far the most common situation, which occurs many thousands of times each trading day, is when shares are traded using the ASX trading facility, the Integrated Trading System (ITS). The ITS is fully computerised so there's no human involvement. You can't directly trade ASX listed shares using the facility because you're not approved by the ASX to do so. To trade shares using the facility you'll need to use the services of a licensed agent, known as a stockbroker.

There are two main types of brokers: offline and online.

Offline brokers

An offline broker is the traditional type of broker: a person with whom you can talk and discuss orders. When you want to trade you usually contact the broker by phone, but you might also send a fax or email.

There are several types of offline brokers that offer different types of services:

⇨ *No advice broker.* You phone, fax or email the broker with your order and the broker arranges the transaction according to your directions.

⇨ *Broker who gives advice.* You can talk to the broker and ask for advice or suggestions about any trade you're contemplating.

⇨ *Full-service broker.* The broker will look after your share portfolio for you, provide advice, trade shares according to your instructions and periodically provide financial statements and summaries.

Some offline brokers provide all types of services that may include an online trading service as well, but some provide only one type of service; for example, the broker may be exclusively a trading broker who gives no advice.

Online brokers

The mushrooming growth of the internet has resulted in an increasing use of online trading. When you trade online you don't deal with a person—the transaction occurs automatically using the online broker's computer program that links you to the ASX trading facility, via what is known as a trading platform. Like offline brokers, some online brokers provide several levels of service. To trade online you need to first become an approved client, after which you'll be able to access the trading platform using your account number and password.

Even though you won't be talking to a person when you trade online, online brokers have a telephone service should you encounter any difficulties. You'll be able to talk to a person to help solve your problem but you won't be able to get any share information or trading advice.

Tip

If you trade online, don't use a trading platform that's more sophisticated than you really need or understand. Start off at the most basic level and graduate to a higher level only after you become thoroughly competent with the basic level and you're convinced that a higher service level would be advantageous.

Brokers' fees

Naturally, brokers (whether online or offline) charge fees. These include:

⇨ a transaction fee, known as brokerage

⇨ an account-keeping/maintenance fee.

As you might expect, the fees will depend upon the level of service you sign up for. The more sophisticated the service level the higher the fees.

Brokerage

Brokerage is based on the value of each parcel of shares traded, with a certain minimum amount for low-value parcels. Usually there's no difference in brokerage between a buy and a sell trade. There's no charge for placing orders; brokerage is charged only if the trade takes place. If you decide to change or cancel an order before the trade takes place, you won't incur a charge for doing so.

Tip
Because of the minimum charge, brokerage cost per share increases as the parcel value reduces, so it's not economical to trade shares with parcel values that are too small.

Example 1
Determine the break-even point and therefore minimum economical parcel values with common offline and online brokerage charges as follows:

Offline broker
Brokerage = 1% of the parcel value with a minimum
of $50.

Online broker
Brokerage = 0.2% of parcel value with a minimum
of $20.

Solution
Offline broker: The break-even point is a parcel value of **$5000**, because 1% of $5000 is $50. So it's most economical to trade parcel values of $5000 or more.

Online broker: The break-even point is a parcel value of **$1000**, because 0.2% of $1000 is $20. So it's most economical to trade parcel values of $1000 or more.

Tip
If you want to trade small-value parcels of shares, use an online broking service.

Account-keeping/maintenance fee
Some brokers charge a fee regardless of how often you trade. These fees are common with offline brokers (especially if you're requesting a high level of service) but they're not

so common with online brokers. These account-keeping/ maintenance charges can be levied on a monthly, quarterly, half-yearly or yearly basis and will depend upon the level of service provided.

Tip

Before you register as a customer with a broker, whether online or offline, make sure you fully understand all fees associated with the service.

Settlement period

The ASX has a T+3 settlement period, meaning that funds will be transferred into or out of your account three business days after the day the share trade occurs.

Tip

If you are buying shares, make sure the money required to pay for them (including brokerage) is available in your account three business days after the transaction occurs. As it may take some time to transfer funds from one account to another, it's safest to make sure the money is available in your account when you place a purchase order.

Should you trade offline or online?

A full comparison of the relative benefits and detriments of trading offline or online can be found in my book *Online Investing on the Australian Sharemarket*. In a nutshell, the main advantages of trading online are:

⇨ you have quick and easy access to heaps of information on a 24/7 basis

⇨ you pay lower fees

⇨ you have sole control over your trading decisions.

Many online brokers have no fees other than brokerage on shares traded, so if you're a registered customer you can access all the information available on their website without trading and you won't incur any costs. This usually includes a great deal of past financial information over many years as well as charting and technical analysis tools (such as moving averages). You're usually able to access company announcements and press releases, and in some cases you can also obtain future projections and analysts' recommendations.

Tip

It's not that difficult to trade online and I strongly suggest you give it a go, but if you've never done so before you should refer to my online investing book for further essential information and advice. If you're not confident that you'll be able to trade competently online, one approach is to set yourself up with an online broker and then start out in a small way, making low-value trades until you become more confident.

Setting up with an offline broker

There are many licensed offline brokers operating in Australia. You will want to use one that is conveniently contactable; the *Yellow Pages* should provide a good starting point. You'll need to make initial contact with the broker and discuss your situation and the type of service you want. The broker will advise you on brokerage and other charges (if applicable) and what you'll need to do if you want to become a client. If you want trading or investment advice, the broker will want to know your risk profile, financial situation and goals. You'll most likely need to fill out an application form or have a personal interview. Before the broker trades shares on your behalf, you'll need to negotiate how you'll pay for any shares purchased and how you'll be paid for any shares sold. You may need to set up a dedicated share trading account that the broker can access, depending on how often you intend to trade.

Choosing an online broker

If you decide to trade online, your first step is to decide which online broking service you'll use. There are approximately 20 online brokers operating in Australia, and most are owned by or affiliated with a bank or finance company. The big four banks—Commonwealth, Westpac, NAB and ANZ— all provide an online trading service, and so do some of the smaller, regional financial institutions such as Suncorp.

There's a detailed comparison of the various online brokers operating in Australia in chapter 4 of my book *Online Investing on the Australian Sharemarket*.

Tip

It may be advantageous to use an online trading service affiliated with the bank you use for your day-to-day banking transactions as transfers of funds into or out of your share trading account may be quicker, easier and cheaper (or free).

Setting up with an online broker

Once you've decided which online broker to use, you need to make contact one way or another and obtain an application form. Then it's just a matter of providing the necessary information and identification. You'll need to stipulate a bank account that can be used for share transactions and give the broker authority to withdraw and deposit funds for the trades you make. You'll be given an account number or log in to access the website in conjunction with your password.

The most popular online broker in Australia is CommSec, affiliated with the Commonwealth Bank, which administers about 1.4 million accounts and averages about 30 000 online trades per day.

Tip

The account number for your online trading account is usually different to the account number of your share funds bank account, so make sure you identify which is which. I've written my online share trading account number on a small sticker and pasted it on the border of my computer screen.

The CommSec website is user-friendly and contains many financial statistics and technical indicators. You have the option of opening a dedicated share trading account — known as a direct investment account — if you want to. You need an initial cash deposit of at least $5000, and once you've set up the account you'll be able to trade at the so-called internet-preferred rate, which is only $19.95 for parcels in value up to $10 000. There's no minimum balance on the account so once you've deposited funds you can spend almost all the money in the account and still qualify for the internet-preferred rate when you trade.

Tip

If you become a customer with an online broker you can access all the information on the website and you don't even need to trade. Many online brokers, such as Comm-Sec, have no account-keeping fees, so it's worthwhile to become a registered customer even if you don't trade.

CHESS

When you first register with a broker, you'll be asked if you want to be sponsored by them in the Clearing House Electronic Sub-register System, known as CHESS. Without going into a detailed analysis of CHESS, the short answer is: join. It's one of those rare things in life that's advantageous for you with no significant disadvantages. You'll be given a holder identification number (HIN), and it's the same for all shares you buy or sell using that broker. You'll be sent a CHESS statement for all shares you own, and a new statement whenever your shareholding changes.

The way CHESS is set up, if you buy a parcel of shares with one broker you can't sell those shares using another broker as the HIN will be different. Despite this, you don't have to trade with a single broker as you can transfer shares from one broker to another without any cost to you. The broker you're transferring to will arrange the transfer at your request.

Tip
For a more detailed discussion of CHESS, please refer to either of my other two share investing books.

Stock codes

The companies or stocks listed on the ASX are each given a unique code consisting of three capital letters. For example, the code for Commonwealth Bank is CBA, Woolworths is WOW and BHP Billiton is BHP. For listed investment instruments other than ordinary stocks (such as options, warrants and hybrids), the code will consist of up to six letters. It's important to know the codes of stocks you are interested in (particularly if you trade using the internet), because it's the way stocks and other investment instruments are identified in the ASX trading system. Some financial publications provide the codes, and you can easily find them on the internet; for example, on the ASX website or online trading sites.

As well as stock codes, the ASX also identifies market indices (such as the All Ords index) with a three-letter code. For example, the All Ords code is XAO. Also the various market sectors are given the same type of code; for example, the energy sector is XEJ. You'll find market and sector codes listed in some financial publications and on the internet, and my book *Online Investing on the Australian Sharemarket* has a complete listing and description of them.

Tip

Keep a list of important codes in a convenient place. This will save you hunting for codes whenever you want to trade or research.

Chapter summary

⇨ Like any tradeable commodity you can transfer ownership of shares via an agreed contract between one party and another, but the vast majority of shares are bought and sold using the ASX Integrated Trading System.

⇨ You can't trade directly using the ASX trading facility: you need to use the services of a licensed broker when you want to buy or sell shares.

⇨ There are two main types of brokers: online and offline.

⇨ All brokers charge a fee known as brokerage that's calculated as a proportion of the parcel value of a trade, with a certain minimum charge for low-value parcels.

⇨ Some brokers (particularly offline ones) levy a charge whether or not you trade, and you need to investigate any such charges before you become a registered client with any broker.

⇨ You generally use an offline broker when you want to discuss proposed trades with an expert and you want some advice.

⇨ If you use an online broker you trade without human contact so you're totally in control of all your trading decisions. Online trading has the lowest fees and gives you quick and easy access to heaps of information on a 24/7 basis.

⇨ If you become a registered client with an online broker you're able to access the information on their website and that's a big advantage.

⇨ Whether you trade online or offline it may be advantageous to set up a dedicated share trading account.

⇨ When shares are bought and sold, the cash transfer occurs three working days after the day of the transaction.

⇨ When you become a registered client with a broker you'll be asked if you want to join CHESS, and I suggest you do so.

⇨ When the broker sponsors you into CHESS, you'll be allocated a unique holder identification number for all the shares you purchase with the broker.

⇨ When you buy shares using one broker, you can't sell these shares using another broker, as the HIN will be different. However, you can transfer shares from one broker to another at no cost to you.

⇨ All listed stocks and indices have a unique three-letter code that you need to know to trade online or when you want to chart a stock or index.

⇨ It saves time to keep all codes of interest in a convenient place for quick access.

chapter 17

Putting the plan into action

In previous chapters I have outlined the basic principles of sound long-term share investing for growth and profitability. In this chapter I look at how you can put the plan into action to build a solid share portfolio.

Investing criteria list

The first step is to establish a set of share investing criteria based on fundamentals. You can regard this set of criteria as a 'health test' for stocks because you want a portfolio with financially healthy stocks and you need to weed out any unhealthy ones.

Tip

A documented criteria list will help you be more objective and dispassionate in your decision-making.

Each investor has his or her own financial resources, goals and requirements, so it's not feasible to set up a generic list that suits everyone. However, to help you set up your list I've included a sample list that you can use if you want, or modify according to your own needs.

Tip

When setting up your list, you don't want to include too many criteria. It's generally better to have a short list rather than a long one. Simplicity is better than complexity.

Essential criteria

In the interests of simplicity I'll use only four essential criteria in my sample list. I've chosen the following:

⇨ The PE ratio is within ±5 points of the traditional average market PE of about 16 to 17; that is, the PE is in the range 11 to 22.

⇨ The grossed-up dividend yield is at least 5%.

⇨ The debt to equity ratio (DE) is less than 100% and preferably less than 80%.

⇨ The share price is not in a downtrend as indicated by a 70-day SMA on a five-year chart.

Using this PE range automatically means that the companies must be making a profit because if they're operating at a loss there won't be a PE shown. You can be less critical about a PE below the minimum than a PE above it.

For me, for the reasons I've outlined in previous chapters, dividend yield is an important consideration, but some financial analysts take the opposing stance. You need to decide whether to include yield in your criteria list.

Applying the criteria

I will apply the criteria to shares in the top ASX listed companies by market cap, often called leading stocks. I want a portfolio consisting of well-established Australian companies with well-known products that have good market acceptance. If the company has a high market cap this requirement will usually be met automatically, but there are some exceptions with companies that operate primarily overseas (even though they're listed on the ASX). You might want to weed these out.

At the time of writing there were about 1250 ASX listed industrial stocks and 800 ASX listed mining stocks, making a total of over 2000. This is a formidable quantity to troll through, but since stocks in the top of the range by market cap are the only ones to be considered the task is much easier. Many newspapers and magazines have a listing of leading stocks in market cap order. For example, Saturday's *Sydney Morning Herald* publishes a list of the top 150 companies updated to the close of trading the previous Friday evening. Using a list like this as a starting point, most stocks are eliminated and there's a far more convenient number to consider.

In the *Sydney Morning Herald* list there are 16 columns of financial data. I've listed these below with my explanation in brackets where necessary. Reading from left to right they are:

⇨ position this week (ranking by market cap)

⇨ position last week

⇨ market cap $m

⇨ last sale (at close of trade on the previous trading day)

⇨ 12-month high (highest trade price for the previous 12 months)

⇨ 12-month low (lowest trade price for the previous 12 months)

⇨ change on week (price change during the week in cents)

⇨ price/NTA (ratio of price to net tangible assets per share)

⇨ price/BV (ratio of price to book value of assets per share)

⇨ EPS (earnings per share in cents)

⇨ PE (price to earnings ratio)

⇨ DPS (dividend per share in cents)

⇨ dividend yield as a percentage

⇨ gross yield (grossed-up yield)

⇨ TSR 1 yr (total shareholder return for the last year as a percentage of the last sale price)

⇨ TSR 3 yr (total shareholder return for the last three years as a percentage of the last sale price).

If you're using financial data that doesn't show grossed-up yield, the yield needs to be at least 3.5% if fully franked or 5% unfranked.

Total shareholder return is the sum of the dividends received and the capital gains for the period under consideration. So the TSR 1 yr is the total percentage return on the shares had they been bought a year ago. The TSR 3 yr is the total percentage return on the shares had they been bought three years ago.

Preliminary screening

The 16 bits of data for each company are useful (particularly the TSR), but there's too much information for a preliminary screening. Initially I'll focus on only two columns: the PE and the dividend yield.

Tip

To screen easily from a list of shares I suggest you use a ruler and a red pen and rule red lines down the columns of interest.

Example 1

As an example of the procedure, I used the *Sydney Morning Herald* share list at the beginning of 2010 to perform an initial screening. In only 15 minutes I was able to troll through the list of 150 top companies using the PE and GUY (grossed-up yield) criteria and come up with a shortlist of only 25 stocks that satisfied both criteria. Unfortunately the *Sydney Morning Herald* list doesn't give the ASX code for each company; I used the share list published in the *Financial Review Smart Investor* magazine to obtain the codes. This took another 10 minutes, so this part of the exercise took less than half an hour. The initial shortlist I came up with is shown in table 12.1. It's in order according to market cap.

Table 12.1: initial shortlist

Rank	Company	Code	PE	GUY %	DE %	Chart
2	CBA	CBA	16.1	6.16		
3	Westpac	WBC	18.7	7.05		
10	Wesfarmers	WES	18.3	5.36		
11	Woolworths	WOW	18.0	5.48		
13	QBE Insurance	QBE	11.5	5.61		
19	AMP	AMP	22.0	5.96		
27	Brambles	BXB	15.5	5.11		
28	Coca-cola Amatil	CCL	20.7	5.11		
39	ASX	ASX	18.6	6.91		
58	Alumina	AWC	18.0	10.1		
63	Telecom NZ	TEL	11.2	8.4		
71	Metcash	MTS	14.1	8.36		
75	Tattersall's Group	TTS	10.7	12.8		
83	Billabong Intl	BBG	15.4	5.1		
84	David Jones	DJS	16.7	7.62		
89	SP Ausnet Stpld	SPN	11.2	12.5		
91	UGL	UGL	16.3	6.42		
94	Bank of Queensland	BOQ	14.1	6.94		
101	Goodman Fielder	GFF	11.7	7.44		
111	APA Group Stpld	APA	21.0	9.09		
112	WA Newspapers	WAN	19.1	5.87		
117	Adelaide Brighton	ABC	12.5	7.69		
129	Healthscope	HSP	16.7	6.36		
139	Spark Infrastructure Stpld	SKI	17.6	12.1		
149	Premier Invest	PMV	13.2	6.06		

You can draw up the table manually or use a computer table or spreadsheet.

The *Financial Review Smart Investor* shares table isn't a complete list of all ASX stocks. Minor stocks are omitted. This isn't a problem since minor stocks won't be included in the list.

I've included Tattersall's in the list even though the PE is a little below 11 because the grossed-up yield is so good.

Several in the list are stapled securities. These are stocks that have been split into separate entities but for trading purposes the various entities are combined into a single tradeable instrument. This need not concern you other than to note that the dividend may be split into several categories that may have a different tax treatment (for example, there may be a capital gains component).

You might want to eliminate some companies from your shortlist on the grounds that they don't operate primarily in Australia. For example, Telecom NZ or Brambles might be omitted for this reason.

The list is current only at the time it is compiled. As share prices change or companies announce changes in earnings or dividends, the companies in the list will most likely change.

Tip

When compiling your table, leave two blank columns on the right as I've shown so you can insert the DE and chart criteria later on.

DE criteria

The next step is to look at companies in the shortlist and ensure that they conform to the DE criteria (debt to equity ratio); that is, to be below 100% (and preferably below 80%). The *Sydney Morning Herald* major stocks list doesn't give this information, so it's necessary to look elsewhere. A great place to search is an online broking site. To access the information on the site, you need to be registered and have a log in number and password.

As the CommSec site is far and away the most popular broker site in Australia, I'll use this for my example. After logging in you'll be at the home page—you can type in the three-letter code of the stock you're researching. So for the first one in the shortlist, Commonwealth Bank, you'll type in CBA, and this will take you to the market depth screen. At the time of writing, this screen for CBA was as shown in figure 12.1.

Figure 12.1: CommSec market depth screen

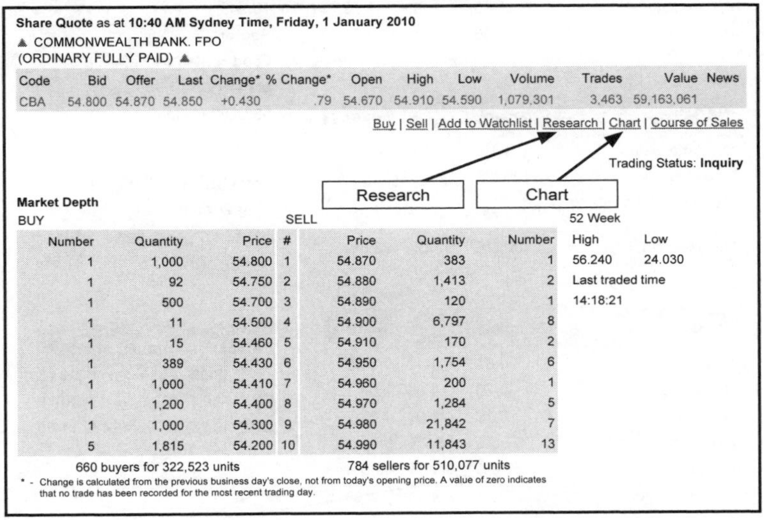

Share Quote as at **10:40 AM Sydney Time, Friday, 1 January 2010**
▲ COMMONWEALTH BANK. FPO
(ORDINARY FULLY PAID) ▲

Code	Bid	Offer	Last	Change*	% Change*	Open	High	Low	Volume	Trades	Value	News
CBA	54.800	54.870	54.850	+0.430	.79	54.670	54.910	54.590	1,079,301	3,463	59,163,061	

Buy | Sell | Add to Watchlist | Research | Chart | Course of Sales

Trading Status: **Inquiry**

Market Depth

BUY / SELL

Number	Quantity	Price	#	Price	Quantity	Number
1	1,000	54.800	1	54.870	383	1
1	92	54.750	2	54.880	1,413	2
1	500	54.700	3	54.890	120	1
1	11	54.500	4	54.900	6,797	8
1	15	54.460	5	54.910	170	2
1	389	54.430	6	54.950	1,754	6
1	1,000	54.410	7	54.960	200	1
1	1,200	54.400	8	54.970	1,284	5
1	1,000	54.300	9	54.980	21,842	7
5	1,815	54.200	10	54.990	11,843	13

660 buyers for 322,523 units   784 sellers for 510,077 units

52 Week

High	Low
56.240	24.030

Last traded time
14:18:21

* - Change is calculated from the previous business day's close, not from today's opening price. A value of zero indicates that no trade has been recorded for the most recent trading day.

Source: www.CommSec.com.au

This screen is the one you use if you want to trade as it summarises the trading action including last sale price, number of shares traded and number of buyers and sellers with bid prices (buy prices) and offer prices (sell prices). For research purposes the trading data isn't relevant; we want the *Research* and *Chart* links that I've highlighted in figure 12.1.

The *Research* tab links you to the main view page (default page). This page contains the following ten tabs: *Main view*,

Forecasts, Financials, Company info, News, Announcements, Analysis, Dividends, Shareholders, Directors.

If you click on the *Financials* tab, you'll see a table like the one shown in figure 12.2 for Woolworths (WOW).

Figure 12.2: Woolworths key measures

Key Measures Woolworths (WOW)

VALUE	Company	All Ords	Sector
P/E ratio	16.94	14.20	17.91
P/B ratio	4.82	1.47	1.57
P/E Growth ratio	1.55	1.99	1.55
P/S ratio	0.66	1.72	0.53

INCOME	Company	All Ords	Sector
Dividend yield	4.1%	4.5%	4.1%
Franking	100.0%		
Tax adjusted dividend yield	3.2%	3.3%	3.2%
Dividend stability	100.0%	92.0%	92.6%

RISK	Company	All Ords	Sector
Beta	0.63	1.10	0.65
Current ratio	0.76	1.61	0.81
Quick ratio	0.19	1.07	0.37
Earnings stability	87.8%	55.2%	55.3%
Debt/Equity ratio	46.6%	34.7%	48.6%
Interest Cover	12.11	4.11	2.14

				DE

GROWTH RATES	10yr	5yr	1yr	2yr Fcst
Sales	9.6%	8.0%	4.5%	
Cashflow	9.4%	11.7%	-2.5%	
Earnings	18.6%	17.6%	12.1%	10.9%
Dividends	18.2%	18.2%	13.0%	9.5%
Book Value	15.4%	22.7%	12.5%	

	Previous Close	52 week high	52 week low
	26.85	30.57	24.36

P/E Ratio
16.94

Sector
Food & Staples Retailing

Market Capital
$33,283 million

Total Shareholder Return
(avg annual rate)

1yr	3yr	5yr	10yr
4.6%	7.4%	15.9%	21.6%

Earnings and Dividends Forecast (cents per share)

	2009	2010	2011	2012
EPS	149.7	168.6	184.1	207.9
DPS	104.0	114.5	124.6	144.0

Source: www.CommSec.com.au

This table contains lots of information, but at this stage only the DE (debt to equity) statistic is relevant. I've highlighted it, and you can see that for Woolworths it is 46.6%. Transfer the DE value to the DE column in the shortlist. (The data on this page is somewhat different from that in table 12.1 because I didn't access this page at the same time that I compiled my shortlist.)

Figure 12.2 doesn't show all the information on the web page; there are some links at the top that don't appear in the table I've reproduced.

As I've pointed out before, the DE statistic isn't meaningful for banking stocks and is not given with the financial data. Also for insurance companies the DE statistic isn't shown; this is because they have large debts in the form of outstanding insurance claims. However, I calculated it from other information, as follows:

QBE:
Long-term debt $2.287 billion
Shareholder equity $6.283 billion
Therefore DE = 2.287 ÷ 6.283 = 0.364 = 36.4%

AMP:
Long-term debt $0.435 billion
Shareholder equity $2.412 billion
Therefore DE = 0.435 ÷ 2.412 = 0.1803 = 18%

Tip

After you've noted the DE statistic, click the New search link at the top of the financials page and type in the next ASX three-letter code in the list. This way you can troll through the list quickly; I was able to go through the 25 stocks in the shortlist in only 15 minutes.

Chart criteria

The final step in completing the shortlist is to check that the price isn't trending downwards. Ideally, the price should be trending up, but if the price is in a sideways pattern with clear support and resistance levels that doesn't eliminate the stock provided, there's no good reason to suspect a price breakout below the support level.

To identify price trends, go back to the market depth screen and click the *Chart* link, which takes you to the charting page. You can then set up the chart parameters you want (such as five-year daily line chart, with 70-day SMA) and obtain a chart similar to the one in figure 12.3 for Brambles (BXB).

Figure 12.3: Brambles chart

Source: www.CommSec.com.au / Wall St on Demand

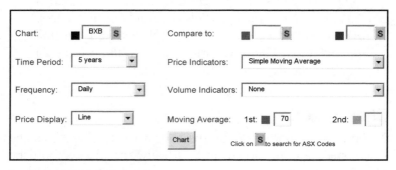

Source: www.CommSec.com.au

You can examine the chart and draw conclusions about the long-term trend. I've concluded that at this time (January 2010) the Brambles price appears to be in a downtrend as indicated by the 70-day SMA. After drawing your own conclusions you can complete the last column of the shortlist. I use the following notation in my list:

⇨ U = uptrend

⇨ D = downtrend

⇨ S = sideways trend.

Tip

Once you've set up the charting parameters, you don't need to set them up again to access the next chart; simply overwrite the code with the next one. This shortcut allowed me to access and examine 25 charts in only 15 minutes.

Eliminated stocks

The following seven stocks were eliminated from the list:

⇨ Brambles, DE = 156.3% and price trend unfavourable

⇨ Coca-Cola Amatil, DE = 175.4%

⇨ Telecom NZ, DE = 98.3% which is high, and price trend unfavourable

⇨ SP Ausnet, DE = 201.6%

⇨ APA Group, DE = 325.4%

⇨ WA Newspapers, DE = 469%

⇨ Spark Infrastructure, DE = 441.3%.

Final shortlist

The final shortlist is 18 stocks, shown in table 12.2.

Table 12.2: final shortlist

Rank	Company	Code	PE	GUY %	DE %	Chart
2	CBA	CBA	16.1	6.16	–	S
3	Westpac	WBC	18.7	7.05	–	S
10	Wesfarmers	WES	18.3	5.36	30.4	U
11	Woolworths	WOW	18.0	5.48	46.6	S
13	QBE Insurance	QBE	11.5	5.61	36.4	S
19	AMP	AMP	22.0	5.96	18.0	S
39	ASX	ASX	18.6	6.91	3.6	S
58	Alumina	AWC	18.0	10.1	37.5	S
71	Metcash	MTS	14.1	8.36	50.5	S
75	Tattersall's Group	TTS	10.7	12.8	35.0	S
83	Billabong Intl	BBG	15.4	5.1	47.4	S
84	David Jones	DJS	16.7	7.62	14.8	S
91	UGL	UGL	16.3	6.42	51.6	S
94	Bank of Queensland	BOQ	14.1	6.94	–	S
101	Goodman Fielder	GFF	11.7	7.44	66.1	S
117	Adelaide Brighton	ABC	12.5	7.69	58.8	S
129	Healthscope	HSP	16.7	6.36	72.9	U
149	Premier Invest	PMV	13.2	6.06	8.3	S

Final selection

You can now make your final selection taking into account the following factors:

⇨ The amount of capital you have available for share investing.

⇨ The number of different stocks you want in your portfolio and therefore the amount of capital invested in each.

⇨ The desired balance of your portfolio, to obtain good diversification in a variety of different sectors.

The 18 companies in the final shortlist are in a variety of sectors, although some stocks are in the same sector. For example, in the banking sector there are three stocks: CBA,

Westpac and Bank of Queensland. Of these, CBA and Westpac are major players whereas Bank of Queensland is a smaller, regional bank. As the banking sector is one of the major sectors in the Australian sharemarket, it wouldn't hurt to have at least one major bank and one regional bank in your portfolio.

Also the list includes several stocks in the retail sector: Woolworths, David Jones and Billabong. Although these companies are in the same sector, there are considerable differences in the nature of their operations, so there's an inherent level of diversification. For example, Billabong specialises in surfwear and, unlike Woolworths and David Jones, has its own production facilities as well as retail outlets.

Additional criteria

The initial selection included only four criteria. To narrow the field further some additional criteria can be considered. For example, you could include the following:

⇨ Price to earnings growth ratio (PEG). This information is shown in figure 12.2 in the 'Value' section. Ideally, you'd like the PEG to be less than 1.0. For Woolworths it's 1.55, which indicates that the share price is higher than can be justified by the expected growth in earnings. You could consider eliminating Woolworths because of this.

⇨ One-year or three-year total shareholder return, as shown in the original newspaper listing of leading stocks. Clearly a company that has produced good shareholder returns over an extended period has a good track record and is preferable to one that doesn't have a good track record.

⇨ Having a dividend reinvestment plan (DRP) available for shareholders. If you're having difficulty making a choice between companies, this might be the final factor to tip the scales. For long-term investing a DRP is a very good feature for the reasons I've outlined in previous chapters.

You can find out whether a DRP is available from the company info page on the CommSec website.

Tip

The company info page on the CommSec website is most useful as it gives a short description of the business and its strategy. An example of this page is shown in figure 12.4. I've highlighted the section telling you whether a DRP is in operation. In the case of QBE, there is one and a 2.5% discount applies. This means that when your dividend is converted to shares, the price at which the shares are allocated to you is discounted by 2.5%.

Divergences

Often when you're trying to decide whether to include a stock in your portfolio you'll come across a divergence. This occurs when all criteria are met except one. For example, a company may have a good PE, a high dividend yield, a good history of shareholder returns and be in an uptrend on the price chart, yet have a higher DE than you'd like. What do you do in a situation like this?

Clearly there's no hard and fast rule and you need to make a decision by weighing up the evidence. If the company is well-established and has a track record of good shareholder returns, you might wonder why a high DE is an obstacle. The answer is that it's not, provided that the business and the economy are healthy. However, as I've previously pointed out, a company with a high DE is inherently more risky if there's a downturn in the economy. For example, during the global financial crisis companies with high DEs were hit hardest and many struggled to survive even in the recovery phase.

Putting the plan into action

Figure 12.4: QBE company profile

Company Profile   Last update: 7 January, 2010   New Search

ASX Code: **QBE**   **QBE Insurance Group Limited**

Main View | Forecasts | Financials | Company Info | News | Announcements | Analysis |
Dividends | Shareholders | Directors

Buy | Sell | Depth | Chart | Watchlist

Qualitative Analysis

Click Here for Company Strategy

Click Here for Company Wrap

Business Description

QBE Insurance Group (QBE) is a leading provider of general insurance and reinsurance services in Australia, the Pacific, Asia, the Americas and Europe. QBE has operations in 45 countries and has made almost 120 successful acquisitions since 1982. QBE is one of the best managed and profitable insurance groups in the global general insurance and reinsurance industry.

Company Strategy

QBEs strategic objective is to remain a highly respected and successful general insurance and reinsurance group by earning underwriting surpluses in each insurance division and country combined with above benchmark investment returns. The objectives of management are to grow shareholder wealth over the long-term while maintaining a sound solvency position and a low risk profile. Extensive risk management is in place to protect all stakeholders. QBEs growth strategy is based on organic growth from existing diversified operations supplemented by astute value-adding acquisitions. Since 1982 QBE has made over 110 acquisitions and currently operates in 45 countries. QBE Insurance Group reported NPAT down 3% to $1.86bn for the year ended 31 December 2008. Revenue from ordinary activities were $15.94bn, up 7% from last year. Diluted EPS was 205.9 cents compared to 217.3 cents last year. Net operating cash flow was $2.25bn compared to $2.37bn last year. The final dividend declared was 65 cents, taking the full year dividend to 126 cents compared with 122 cents last year.

Company Details

QBE Insurance Group Limited

Trading Status: Trading

Former Names:

ACN:008 485 014

Chairman: Edwin (John) Cloney,

MD: Francis OHalloran,

Level 2, 82 Pitt St

Sydney,NSW 2000

Tel:(02) 9375 4444

Fax:(02) 9235 3166

http://www.qbe.com   DRP

Dividend Reinvestment? Yes

2.5% Discount

Shareholder discounts: No

Investor relations phone:--

Principal Registry:
Name: Link Market Services Limited
Level 12, 680 George St
Sydney South, NSW 2000
Telephone: 1300 554 474
Fax: +61 2 8280 7111
Internet:
www.linkmarketservices.com.au
Email:
registrars@linkmarketservices.com.au

Auditors: PricewaterhouseCoopers
Banker: n/a
Solicitor: n/a

Source: www.CommSec.com.au

The *Top Stocks* approach

Before concluding this chapter, I'd like to mention Martin Roth's book *Top Stocks*. It's published every year in early November and retails for about $30. It contains information for around 100 leading stocks selected using Martin's criteria, which are outlined at the beginning of the book. The book provides a lot of useful information in one volume, and in my opinion is a good starting point for research and well worth the modest cost involved.

The financial data and charts are up to date only to 30 June for the previous year, which means that financial data and charts in the 2010 edition are up to date to 30 June 2009. Martin's selection criteria doesn't include price value so he includes many stocks with PEs much higher or lower than I consider acceptable. Also he doesn't take into account the dividend yield or calculate the grossed-up yield, and he includes many stocks with low dividend yields that I'd eliminate on the basis of my dividend yield criteria. Finally, he doesn't include listed investment companies or property trusts; I don't automatically eliminate these if they satisfy the other criteria.

If you have an existing portfolio

So far I've adopted a starting-from-scratch approach assuming that you don't already have a share portfolio. But what if you do have a substantial portfolio of shares, what then? In this case, I suggest the following approach:

⇨ Determine the dollar value of your existing portfolio. Of course, it will vary from day to day but this doesn't matter as you don't need a precise value.

⇨ Add the value of your existing shares to any cash you've set aside for share investing. This now becomes your total available share investing cash pool.

⇨ Decide on the degree of diversification you want; that is, how many different stocks you want to hold. Then you can work out the value allocated to each stock. For example, if your total available cash pool is $100 000 and you'd like to have 10 stocks, each one should have a value of about $10 000.

⇨ Go through the exercise of selecting stocks using the method I've outlined, trying not to put any bias on shares you already own but treating them exactly as you would any others.

⇨ After setting up your ideal portfolio, compare it to your existing one. Does your existing portfolio contain shares you wouldn't buy now if you were starting from scratch, or are there shares missing from it that you want to include?

⇨ Now you can decide if you should continue to hold any shares you wouldn't buy now or if you should sell them and use the funds to purchase shares you would like to hold.

⇨ Finally, you can compare the value of shares you own to the value they should have in your ideal, well-balanced portfolio. If any of the values are too low, consider buying some more shares; if they are too high, consider selling some in order to get a better balance in your portfolio.

Tip

When evaluating your existing portfolio, try to be as dispassionate as you can and not allow emotion to bias your decisions. Wishing and hoping aren't a good basis for decision-making.

Example 2

After setting up your ideal portfolio you look at your existing one and find that you own two stocks, A and B, that don't fit your criteria in the following ways:

⇨ A doesn't conform to most of your criteria.

⇨ B conforms to most of your criteria but the shares have a value of $27 000, and for good balance in your portfolio their value should be $20 000.

What do you do now?

Solution

In this situation, without any mitigating information that could influence your decisions, you could take the following action:

⇨ Stock A: **sell all your shares**. If the price is not trending up and the stock doesn't conform to most of your criteria it has no place in your portfolio.

⇨ Stock B: **sell a $7000 parcel of shares** to bring the value back to $20 000. Although it's a good stock, the shares are overweighted and you can invest the $7000 in other shares and bring your portfolio into balance.

Tip

A good way of evaluating any stock you own is to ask yourself the following question: 'If I didn't own these shares but had their value as dollars in my investment account, would I buy them now?' If the answer to this question is 'no' then sell, unless the price is trending upward, in which case wait until a reversal occurs.

Chapter summary

⇨ To develop a sound portfolio of shares you need to start with a criteria list (or health test). Write down your criteria list and keep it handy in document form.

⇨ Don't have too many essential criteria in your initial list —I suggest about four is fine.

⇨ You can start looking for shares that satisfy your criteria from a list of leading Australian companies; that is, the top 100 or 150 by market capitalisation.

⇨ A market leader list is often given in the financial section of newspapers.

⇨ An initial troll through the list by PE and yield (grossed-up) won't take very long and will reduce the list to a more manageable number.

⇨ You can then look at the DE and share chart of each stock in your list. This information can best be obtained from a website such as CommSec.

⇨ I suggest you eliminate stocks with high debt levels or whose share price is in a downtrend as indicated by a moving average in the range 50 to 100 days on a five-year chart. After you've done this, you should end up with a list of about 20 stocks.

⇨ You can now apply some additional criteria, including price to earnings growth ratio (PEG), total shareholder return and DRP availability.

⇨ Your final selection should take into account the balance of sectors so as to obtain a well-diversified portfolio.

⇨ When a stock satisfies your criteria in all aspects except one, you have to decide whether the divergence is sufficiently important to exclude the stock from your list.

⇨ If you're starting from scratch you can set up your ideal portfolio by purchasing shares included in your shortlist.

⇨ The book *Top Stocks* by Martin Roth is a good resource that screens all listed Australian stocks according to Martin's selection criteria and provides a more manageable level of 100 or so stocks to start your search. However, the selection criteria he uses doesn't include any relevant price/value data such as PE, PEG or dividend yield. The book contains good financial data but it won't be the most recent.

⇨ If you already own shares, compare your existing portfolio to your ideal one and decide what action (if any) you should take so as to more closely align your existing portfolio with your ideal one.

chapter 13

Keeping up to date

After you've set up your portfolio, you need to keep up to date with any developments and maintain proper records. In this chapter I'll discuss the records you should keep and the changes that can occur as time goes on, and how to deal with them.

Keeping stock files

Keeping proper stock records doesn't mean throwing all your CHESS certificates, dividend statements and shareholder information in a shoebox for someone else to sort through some time in the future. A system I use and recommend is to set up a dedicated file for each stock you own. These files could be stored in a metal filing cabinet or an inexpensive concertina-type cardboard file. In the file for each stock, place all relevant information about it, including contract notes, directors' and annual reports, dividend statements, CHESS statements and newspaper articles. If you sell a stock, sort through the file and retain only the information required by the ATO (dividend statements and contract notes) and put these in a 'sold stocks' file.

Tip

When you receive your CHESS statements, before you file them check to make sure that the number of shares shown in the statements exactly matches the number you own according to your records. If there's a discrepancy you need to investigate it, and if you can't find the problem contact the share registry.

Dividend summaries

Each financial year you need to declare any dividends and franking credits in your income tax return, so you need to keep track of them. It's a good idea to have a dividend summary sheet that you keep in each stock file. You can use a sheet of lined paper on which you draw the columns, or you can use a computer table or spreadsheet.

A suggested format for a dividend summary is shown in table 13.1.

Table 13.1: dividend summary

Code	Date	Dividend uf	Dividend franked	Franking credit

The date is the allotment date; that is, the date on which the dividend is transferred to you. This isn't the same as the record date or the ex-dividend date. The record date is the date used by the share registry to determine shareholder eligibility for the dividend and is really of no significance to you. The ex-dividend date is the date from which any shares purchased won't be eligible for payment of the dividend. This date is significant only if you wish to buy some more shares or sell some (or all) of the shares you own.

The code will normally remain the same for each line, but the reason for including it will be made clear when I discuss the master summary.

DRP summary

If you've joined the dividend reinvestment plan (DRP), the table needs to be more comprehensive. A suggested format for these shares is shown in table 13.2.

Table 13.2: DRP summary

Code	Date	Dividend uf	Dividend franked	Franking credit	Shares issued	Issue price	Cost of shares	Total shares	Total cost

This table will be of great value to you (or your beneficiaries) if at any time in the future any shares are sold. As before, the code should remain the same for each line in the table.

This summary is more detailed than the one shown in my book *Teach Yourself About Shares*.

Master dividend summary

As well as keeping a dividend summary (or DRP summary) for each stock you own that pays a dividend, it's a good idea to compile a master dividend summary for your entire portfolio. Keep the master summary in a separate file and update it each time you receive a dividend. A master summary will prove to be a boon when submitting your tax return and also when monitoring profitability of your shares (to be discussed in the next chapter).

For your master summary, compile another table using the format in table 13.1 and include all your shares in it. If you've compiled each dividend summary manually, you'll need to rewrite the information from each individual summary in the master summary. If you've used a computer, all you need to do is set up the master summary as another computer table and copy and paste each individual summary into your master summary. For shares in the DRP, use the same idea but copy and paste the first five columns of table 13.2.

To obtain the dividend information you need for your income tax return or when calculating your profitability, add each of the last three columns of the master summary and obtain totals for the year in question.

Tip

When using a spreadsheet for your dividend summaries, total amounts can be calculated using the sum function. This is quicker and also eliminates calculation errors.

Example 1

As an example I've included an actual dividend statement in figure 13.1 that I'll explain below.

The dividend statement is an interim one for ANZ Bank shares for the half-year ended 31 March 2009. A shareholder continuing to hold the shares will receive a final dividend for the half-year ended 30 September.

The franked amount and the dividend amount are the same because the shares are fully franked.

The issue price of $15.16 includes a 1.5% discount to the average trading price of the shares in the days prior to the ex-dividend date (as determined by the rules of the DRP). Should the shares allocated under the plan be sold at any time in the future, the acquisition cost of these 79 shares is $15.16 each (total cost $1198).

Figure 13.1: dividend reinvestment plan statement

Allotment date: 1 July 2009

Record date: 13 May 2009

Dividend per Share	Participating Shares	Franked Amount	Dividend Amount	Franking Credit
$0.46	2607	$1199.22	$1199.22	$513.95

DRP Account

Credit balance brought forward: $5.79

Total available for reinvestment: $1205.01

Amount applied to the issue of 79 shares at $15.16 each: $1197.64

Credit balance carried forward in the DRP account: $7.37

Shareholding

Number of shares held: 2607

New DRP shares: 79

Total number of shares now held: 2686

The total cost of the shares issued isn't necessarily exactly equal to the dividend because of rounding-off differences. That's because only a whole number of shares can be issued (there can't be fractions of a share). The rounding-off difference (in this case $7.37) is carried forward in the DRP account and is applied to the next dividend.

If at any time in the future all shares are sold, any money in the DRP account will be paid in cash to the shareholder.

Example 2

Transfer the information on the DRP statement to the DRP summary sheet. Prior to receiving the dividend, the total cost of the 2607 shares held (including original purchase cost) was $38 105.

Solution

The completed summary is shown as table 13.3. (The " is used to denote figures previously included in the table but not shown here.)

Table 13.3: completed DRP summary

Code	Date	Dividend uf	Dividend franked	Franking credit	Shares issued	Issue price	Cost of shares	Total shares	Total cost
"	"	"	"	"	"	"	"	2607	$38 105
ANZ	1/7/09	0	$1199	$514	79	$15.16	$1198	2686	$39 303

I round off to the nearest dollar (except for the issue price); it's legitimate to do so as the ATO doesn't require income or costs to be exact to the cent.

Share issues

From time to time, public companies announce share issues. They do this when they would like additional capital and the directors don't want to increase the amount of loan capital. If there's a share issue and you're an eligible shareholder, you'll receive an offer document. This document will state the number of shares you can purchase, the purchase price and the cut-off date (expiry date). You'll also be given additional information containing details of the offer and the reasons for it.

The issue price is the price of each share you take up under the offer. This may be stated in dollars or as a percentage discount to the average closing price of the shares for a certain number of trading days prior to the cut-off date for the offer. In some cases both will apply; for example, the issue price could be given as $1.50 or 10% below the average closing price of the shares on the ASX for five trading days (whichever is lower).

Sometimes you will be given the option of purchasing additional shares over and above your entitlement. However, if the issue is fully subscribed you may not receive all the additional shares you apply for. You may be able to purchase fewer shares than you're entitled to but there'll usually be a minimum number of shares or purchase cost stipulated.

You don't have to participate in the issue if you don't want to. If you don't, your entitlement will lapse and become worthless after the expiry date.

There are two main types of share issues: rights and options.

Rights

Rights are issued to shareholders in proportion to the number of shares held. For example, if you hold 1350 shares in XYZ Company and it's having a 1 for 10 rights issue, you'll be entitled to purchase 135 shares in the issue. Usually the issue is non-renounceable, meaning that the rights aren't listed for trading on the ASX and you can't sell them. In some cases the issue may be renounceable, meaning they'll be listed and you can trade them.

Options

Options are similar to a renounceable rights issue at a stated price, the main difference being that the time to expiry is usually much longer and may be in the order of several years, rather than a month or two.

Tip

Check carefully the expiry date of any share issue. It's the date by which the share registry must receive your completed application and payment. Even if you're one day late, you'll miss out (unless the expiry date is extended). Allow sufficient time for mail to arrive at its destination.

Should you participate in a new share issue?

This is a difficult question to answer but I'll try to provide some guidance. Of course, the first consideration for you is funds availability. If you don't have the cash necessary you won't be able to take up the offer, but if you do have available cash it's generally a good idea to participate provided that the company is sound and profitable and the issue price is at an acceptable discount to the market price. If the company has fallen on difficult times, participating in the offer may not be in your best interest if the additional capital doesn't help the company get out of trouble (you'd be throwing good money after bad). However, that should be a rare situation if the company is a well-established market leader.

Tip

If the company is a profitable market leader it's usually a good idea to participate in the issue (if you can afford to). If it's a second line or more speculative stock the decision is not so clear-cut and you'll need to give it careful consideration. For a more comprehensive discussion about share issues and the effect on the share price, please refer to chapter 7 of my book Teach Yourself About Shares.

Takeovers

In some cases you may hold shares in a company that's taken over by another one (the predator). For example, I own shares in the Commonwealth Bank (CBA) because I originally held shares in Colonial Bank, and Colonial was taken over by CBA. Before a takeover occurs you'll be notified and the directors will usually provide some guidance as to whether they advise you to vote in favour of it. If the directors agree to the takeover it's known as a friendly one, but if the directors are opposed to the takeover it's known as an unfriendly or hostile one.

There are usually several options available to you as a shareholder:

⇨ receiving cash for all your shares

⇨ conversion of your shares into those of the predator company in some predefined ratio

⇨ receiving part cash, part new shares.

What action should you take with a takeover offer?

As a shareholder, initially you'll need to decide whether to vote in favour of the takeover. Usually it's best to adopt the directors' recommendation. If the takeover proceeds, you'll need to select from the alternatives available to you. Like a share issue, there are no clear-cut guidelines other than if the predator is a market leader and you're happy with the company, it's usually a good idea to convert your shares. If you don't want to do so, you can sell your shares on the market prior to the cut-off date or accept the cash offer for your shares (which will save you the brokerage cost of trading). Either way, you can use the proceeds to buy shares in another company that conforms more closely to your criteria.

Splits and consolidations

Occasionally a split or consolidation can occur with shares you hold. In a split, new shares will be issued to you which will replace the existing ones you hold according to some ratio. For example, if there's a 2:1 split and you hold 1000 shares before the split, after the split you'll hold 2000 new shares. Sounds like a good deal, except there's one catch; can you spot it? Inevitably, after the split the share price will drop (in this case by 50%), so if the old shares were trading at $40, the new shares will trade for $20.

A consolidation works the other way around. So if you hold 10 000 shares and there's a 10:1 consolidation, you'll be issued with only 1000 new shares. In this case the price will increase after the consolidation, so if the shares were trading for $1.00 beforehand, they'll now trade for $10.

Splits and consolidations: what should you do?

If the directors propose a split or consolidation, it's generally best to vote in favour of their recommendation. The value of your shareholding won't change as a result. Splits are usually proposed when the share price is getting rather high and the directors feel that the high price may be deterring investors who might otherwise want to buy shares.

Consolidations are usually proposed when the share price is too low and investors might consider the company to be in the 'penny dreadful' category. In some cases there will be a change in name or code after the issue of the new shares, so you need to be aware of this and adjust your records accordingly.

Tip

If you notice a sudden major leap or drop in a share price, it's most likely due to a split or consolidation. However, the change may not be evident on a share price chart because the software used to produce charts usually adjusts the pre-price to be in line with the post-price according to the ratio used.

Share buybacks

When a company has surplus capital available (for example, from accrued profits or from the sale of assets), the directors may decide to use some of this capital to buy back shares. In effect, they're opting to invest in their own company. A buyback can be done off market (by issuing an offer document to existing shareholders allowing them to sell some or all of the shares they own) or on market (by the company purchasing its own shares on the ASX). In the latter case, as a shareholder there's no decision to make as matters are out of your hands. If the buyback is off market, you'll need to decide whether to participate.

Should you participate in an off-market buyback?

If you're a shareholder, a share buyback is good news whether it's off market or on market. Can you see why? The reasons are as follows:

⇨ After the buyback, there's fewer shares on issue and therefore those held by shareholders become more valuable.

⇨ The buyback is a sign of director confidence in the company.

⇨ The company must be making good profits and be well cashed up.

⇨ There's no brokerage involved if you decide to participate.

As a long-term shareholder, my suggestion is that you don't participate in an off-market buyback. Why sell shares in a profitable company that will most likely be more valuable after the buyback?

Tip

The saving in brokerage in an off-market buyback isn't a major consideration, especially if you can trade online at low brokerage rates.

Chapter summary

⇨ Proper recordkeeping is an essential part of share investing.

⇨ Keep a dedicated file for each stock you own and file all relevant information about that stock in the file.

⇨ Compile a dividend summary (or DRP summary) for each stock you own and keep it in the stock file. Update these each time you receive a dividend.

⇨ Compile a master dividend summary and file it in a separate file. Transfer information from each dividend summary on to the master summary each time you receive a dividend.

⇨ Using a computer spreadsheet for dividend summaries eliminates manual number crunching and avoids calculation errors.

⇨ Companies that require additional capital may issue additional shares, either as a rights issue or an option issue.

⇨ As a shareholder in a renounceable issue, you're able to sell your rights or options on the sharemarket if you wish to do so. If the issue is non-renounceable, you cannot.

⇨ It's generally a good idea to participate in a share issue if the company is a sound one and doesn't need the additional capital just to remain viable. There's no obligation on you to take up rights or options, but if you don't they'll expire worthless after the expiry date.

⇨ Sometimes there may be an attempt by a company to take over another company in which you hold shares. In such cases it's generally best to go along with the directors' recommendations.

⇨ If shares you hold are split or consolidated, the number of shares you hold will change but not the value of your shareholding. All you need to do in such cases is adjust your records accordingly.

⇨ If there's a share buyback in a stock you hold, it's good news and indicates a profitable and well-cashed-up company. It's generally best not to participate in an off-market buyback as the shares you own should become more valuable after the buyback.

chapter 14

Into the future

You've set up your share portfolio and you're maintaining proper records and keeping track of changes and developments. Is there anything else you should do as time goes on? In this chapter I'll look at this question and the decisions and actions that may be necessary.

Monitoring your portfolio

As well as keeping track of your investments and maintaining efficient records, you should keep an eye on the performance of companies you own—a process that's known as monitoring. You need to decide how often you will monitor your portfolio and how you will do so.

How often should you monitor your portfolio?

Short-term traders need to watch the market and their shares constantly. As a long-term investor you don't need to monitor your portfolio so frequently but you still need to do so on a regular basis. If you can spare the time, doing so weekly is a good idea, otherwise I suggest you do so at least once a month.

How should you monitor your portfolio?

If you trade online, your broker will most likely have a facility that automatically tracks your portfolio for you. After you've bought shares you may need to insert the buy cost per share yourself, but after that the portfolio should automatically update with current prices and numbers of shares held. The online portfolio will show the capital gain or loss for each parcel of shares as well as the total for your portfolio.

If you trade online, the first step in the monitoring process is to log in to your broker's website and check the latest value of each parcel of shares in your portfolio and compare this with the values when you previously checked.

Unfortunately, your online portfolio is only a guide to profit and won't provide an accurate figure. It will understate profit as dividends won't be included. Also, if you've joined the DRP or buy shares in the same stock in separate parcels at different times you can't get an accurate capital gain figure from your online portfolio. This is because an online portfolio amalgamates all your shares in a stock and requires you to insert a single buy cost. Actually each parcel of shares bought at different times or received through the DRP will have a different acquisition cost and therefore a different capital gain.

If you don't trade online you'll need to prepare your own portfolio table manually or using a computer spreadsheet. If you intend to use a spreadsheet, there's a sample in *Teach Yourself About Shares* (figure 14.3).

Tip

Whether you use an online spreadsheet facility or compile your own, it's a good idea to keep a hard copy of your portfolio each time you check it in a dedicated file. This provides a permanent record that you can refer to any time in the future.

Monitoring price trends

After checking the value of your share portfolio, the next step in the monitoring process is to look at the price trend of each of your shares. The best way of doing this is to use a chart as it's very difficult to get a feeling for trends from rows of figures. Online brokers have charting facilities available for customers, but if you aren't trading online you can use the ASX site or other free sites that provide charting facilities. You can usually set up the chart in the format you want, and then scroll through your portfolio list and chart each of your shares by overwriting the three-letter code. When doing this it's best to use a relatively short-term chart—I suggest a one-year or six-monthly chart.

Some sites (including the ASX site) don't allow you to customise the chart according to your requirements.

Tip
Details of free sites that have a charting facility are given in my online investing book.

Reviewing your portfolio

It's also a good idea to review or evaluate your portfolio on a regular basis. With your regular monitoring you're checking what's been happening; when you review you're deciding whether you need to take any action, and if so what you should do.

When reviewing your portfolio, possible strategies available to you include:

⇨ Do nothing.

⇨ Buy more shares in a stock you own.

⇨ Sell some (or all) of the shares in a stock you own and use the money to buy shares in a stock you don't own.

When and how often should you review your portfolio?

I suggest that you carry out two types of reviews over two different time frames:

⇨ review as you regularly monitor your portfolio

⇨ conduct long-term performance reviews.

Reviewing as you monitor

When you check the chart for each stock in your portfolio you need to review trends. The charts may show that some of your shares are in a downtrend as indicated by the moving average.

If only one or two of the stocks you own are going down when the rest are going up or moving sideways it's not a good sign, and you need to decide if you want to sell some or all of these shares. If all shares are in a downtrend, it's most likely that the entire sharemarket is in a downtrend, and you can't do anything about that unless you decide to sell your entire shareholding.

Tip

Before you chart each stock in your portfolio, it's a good idea to form an impression of price movements for the market as a whole. The best way of doing this is to chart the All Ords index; you can do so using the code XAO.

Longer term performance reviews

In addition to reviewing as you monitor your shares, I suggest you carry out a more comprehensive review on a six-monthly or annual basis. In this review you calculate profit/loss over the period, including both capital gains and dividends. You can then calculate your return on capital invested and compare it to the target for each parcel of shares you own or that you've traded during the period in question.

Tip

I suggest your annual or six-monthly reviews should match the financial year; that is, 1 July to 31 December (interim period) and 1 January to 30 June (final period).

The longer term performance review can be rather complex if you have a comprehensive portfolio with a significant number of stocks, but it's well worthwhile doing. You can use a spreadsheet to take the pain out of the number crunching.

Tip

Examples of profit/loss and return on capital calculations are given in both of my other share investing books. In addition, a sample spreadsheet with formulas included is given in my online investing book.

When should you sell?

For short-term traders, this question has a rather straight-forward answer that follows from the trading strategy I've outlined in previous chapters: let profits run as long as a favourable trend continues, and sell as soon as there's an adverse change in trend.

Many short-term traders use stop-loss orders, so the sell decision becomes an automatic trade that requires no further input once they've set up the order with the parameters they want. Some traders also place profit stop orders (another type of conditional order), where shares are automatically sold once they reach the preset profit target. However, it's not a trading strategy I advocate.

Tip

Stop-loss orders are the most common type of conditional order and are discussed in detail in each of my other two share investing books. It's worthwhile becoming familiar with them.

For a long-term investor, the sell decision is a most difficult and vexing one, so if you're often agonising about it don't think you're Robinson Crusoe. If you adopt a bottom drawer approach (outlined shortly), you may never sell. You simply hang on and ride the ups and downs without taking any action. However, it seems downright foolish to hang on to shares if they're clearly in a downtrend due to a significant adverse change in fortunes. As I pointed out in the first chapter of this book, according to the efficient market theory the market is always right, and if the price is in a downtrend it's almost always because the market believes a downturn in profitability will occur, either in the immediate future or in the longer term. Clearly a downturn in profitability isn't good news for a long-term investor if it's likely to be sustained. So the question really boils down to whether you believe the downturn is just a blip on the radar or whether it's more serious and long lasting.

To resolve this question you need to research further. The best way of doing this is to look for any company announcements that shed light on any significant changes that have occurred or are likely in the future. Many websites provide access to company announcements, including the ASX site. Usually there'll be an indicator (such as an exclamation mark) alongside the announcement if it is considered to be one that could affect the share price.

Tip

Whenever you notice a significant change in a trend on a chart it's a good idea to check the company announcements to see if you can find an explanation for the change.

Another way you can research significant events that could explain trend changes is to look for relevant news articles published around the time of the change. As you most likely don't have the time or inclination to read right through the financial papers each day, the best way of finding these articles is through online research. Some online broking sites (such as the CommSec site) have links to press releases in the 'company research' section of the site. If there are any relevant press releases, a short synopsis is given.

Tip

News articles are well worthwhile checking, as they provide information that could explain trend changes in a way that's easy to understand.

If your research indicates a significant adverse change in fortunes has taken place or is likely in the future, you need to evaluate whether the shares in question still conform to your selection criteria and whether the change is likely to be a permanent one. If the shares no longer conform to your criteria, consider selling, particularly if you could use the proceeds to buy other shares that do conform to your criteria and therefore would be a better long-term investment.

If your research doesn't shed any light on the causes of the trend change, you're really in the dark. Unfortunately, despite all the financial rules and regulations designed to ensure transparency and to avoid insider trading, there's still information out there that only a limited number of people are privy to and that isn't made public and accessible to ordinary investors. In such cases you can't make an objective decision; you have to rely on your own judgement.

Tip

Trend changes always have an underlying cause but you mightn't always be able to determine what it is.

If you have a stockbroker or investment adviser you can consult, he or she may have some information that you don't so it could be worthwhile getting a second opinion. Bear in mind that stockbrokers and investment advisers who receive a fee when you trade have a vested interest in encouraging you to trade. I'm not suggesting that they're not completely ethical, but at the same time, if you don't trade they don't make money.

Selling and buying back

If you're holding a stock that's basically sound but the shares are moving into a downtrend, another approach you can consider is to sell and buy back: you sell at the start of the downtrend and buy back when the downtrend reverses and an uptrend starts again. As an example of this approach, if you study figure 10.7 on page 139, if you owned CBA shares you could have sold after point B at a price around $55 to $60 when the moving average clearly indicated a trend reversal. The best time to have bought back would have been after point E at around $30, when the downtrend clearly reversed and was replaced by a strong uptrend. As you can see, an investor using the sell and buy back approach would have obtained considerable extra capital gain compared to an investor who simply held CBA shares throughout.

While the sell and buy back approach is basically sound in theory, you need to consider a few factors that might temper your enthusiasm. They are as follows:

⇨ It's very easy to apply the approach with the wisdom of hindsight but far more difficult to do so in real time when looking toward the future. For example, if you study figure 10.7 again, you might have sold prior to point A when the moving average indicated a change from uptrend to downtrend. That would have been disastrous as the price quickly recovered and a long uptrend became established. And what would you have done after point C when the moving average downtrend reversed and seemed to be indicating a new uptrend? Indeed for nearly a year between points C and D the moving averaged bounced around before a downtrend initiated once more.

⇨ When you sell you trigger capital gains tax obligations that could considerably reduce the profitability of the sell and buy back strategy.

⇨ By the time the moving average clearly indicates a downtrend, the price at which you can sell may have dropped considerably from the high, and by the time it indicates an uptrend again the price may have risen considerably from the low. The price differential between your sell price and your buyback price may not be sufficient to make the exercise worthwhile, when you take into account capital gains tax and trading costs.

⇨ In the period of time between selling and buying back you won't be eligible for dividends or share issues.

Tip

A sell and buy back approach can increase capital gains, but after selling, don't be tempted to buy back until an uptrend becomes clearly established.

The bottom drawer approach

A bottom drawer approach is essentially a set-and-forget approach to long-term share investing. It's based on the principle that if you've set up a good, balanced portfolio with sound stocks, you need take no action as time goes on. The term 'bottom drawer' stems from the idea that you simply file your share certificates in the bottom drawer of your filing cabinet where they'll be out of sight and out of mind. The logic behind this approach is that when you buy shares in a company, you're really buying into that company and becoming a part owner. If you've bought a good business that's operating profitably, would you want to sell it because short-term fluctuations in economic conditions affect the value of the business? I think you'd believe that every business periodically experiences periods of higher and lower profitability. A downturn in profitability wouldn't constitute a sound reason for selling the business if you expected that a recovery would occur in the not too distant future.

In chapter 1, I mentioned Warren Buffett, who's widely regarded as the world's best long-term investor. His investing philosophy is essentially a bottom drawer approach. He uses a set of criteria that he's developed and he applies them diligently when seeking companies to invest in, and he seldom sells once he's bought.

As I pointed out previously, all economies go through up and down periods. The so-called economic clock is often used to depict this economic cycling. The period of the cycle—that is, the time between one high and the next (or one low and the next)—has historically been between eight and eleven years. The sharemarket is a prime indicator of the state of the economy and it reacts very quickly to changes in economic conditions. The value of a diversified portfolio of shares in major companies will, by its very nature, fluctuate more or less in step with the sharemarket as a whole. If you expect that these fluctuations will occur, clearly a downturn in the value of shares that's in step with a general market downturn doesn't justify selling unless some change has occurred in the company that will have a long-lasting effect on its performance and profitability.

Advantages of the bottom drawer approach

The advantages of the bottom drawer approach include:

⇨ It's a 'stress less' approach where you don't need to worry about what's happening in the sharemarket in the short term (or even in the medium term).

⇨ Frequent trading has been shown to be a wealth hazard; investors who keep chopping and changing often make less profit than those that sit tight.

⇨ It requires very little input once you've set up your share portfolio. That's to say, you don't need to expend much time or effort on the sharemarket. This is great if you have family or work commitments and limited time available to spend on shares.

⇨ It would require a major event or change in business direction to prompt you to sell good-quality shares.

⇨ Fewer trades means less brokerage.

⇨ If you don't sell, you don't have to pay capital gains tax on profitable shares and thereby reduce the value of your invested capital.

Disadvantages of the bottom drawer approach

The disadvantages of the bottom drawer approach include:

⇨ If you apply it without modification you can find yourself holding shares that just keep going down in value, with your losses increasing until eventually the shares may become worthless. This is an extremely unlikely scenario with market-leading shares but more likely with second line or speculative shares.

⇨ A sell and buy back approach can at times produce superior capital gains compared to a simple buy and hold strategy.

Tip

Never use a bottom drawer approach for second line or speculative shares. (While I try to avoid using the word 'never' in this book, this is one time when the word is applicable.)

As time goes on, some shares in your portfolio will increase in value more than others so your portfolio will become unbalanced. If you take no action, this increases risk as your portfolio will be more concentrated in some sectors.

To summarise, if a company is a market leader and isn't undergoing any major downturn in fortunes, the bottom drawer approach is basically sound for long-term investing in this business.

Chapter summary

⇨ Check on the shares in your portfolio on a regular basis, at least once a month.

⇨ Most online brokers have a portfolio facility that automatically keeps track of your portfolio, but you may need to insert buy prices manually.

⇨ An online portfolio provides a guide to capital gains but understates real profits, as dividends won't be included.

⇨ If you're in a DRP, it's difficult to obtain true capital gains from an online portfolio as the buy cost of each parcel received will be different.

⇨ Examining the chart of each stock in your portfolio is an essential part of the monitoring process.

⇨ When monitoring your portfolio, use a relatively short-term time frame for the chart (six or twelve months is best).

⇨ Review your portfolio regularly. Compare actual performance to your targets and decide if you need to take any action. You can review your portfolio as you monitor it.

⇨ When reviewing, be especially alert for a move to a downtrend in one or more of your stocks when the market as a whole isn't moving down.

⇨ The easiest way to check market performance is by looking at the chart of the All Ords index; you can do so using the code XAO.

⇨ A good way of researching causes is to access company announcements and news items (if any).

⇨ In addition to reviewing as you monitor, it's a good idea to carry out a longer term performance review every twelve months, or preferably every six months.

⇨ If your reviewing indicates that any shares in your portfolio aren't meeting your goals, you need to decide whether you should sell them and buy other shares instead.

⇨ The sell or hold decision is a difficult one for long-term share investors, as there's no clear-cut strategy that's best in all circumstances.

⇨ When trying to decide whether to sell or hold, it's a good idea to try to establish a cause for any trend change you notice and establish whether it's due to a permanent or temporary downturn in profitability.

⇨ The ASX website allows you to access company announcements, and most online broking sites have links to them in the research section.

⇨ A strategy you can consider is to sell and buy back later. If you sell at a relatively high price and buy back at a lower price, this strategy produces higher capital gains than a simple hold strategy, but there are some risks that you need to be aware of.

⇨ A bottom drawer approach is based on the principle that if you've built up a portfolio of good-quality, market-leading stocks, you'll make good profits in the long run without needing to chop and change.

⇨ The bottom drawer approach should never be applied to the more speculative types of shares, but can be used with caution as a basis for investing in market-leading shares provided that there's been no adverse change in fortunes that will permanently affect operations or profitability.

Index